# SEX

# AND
# MORALITY

## ANSWERS FOR
## MODERN CATHOLICS

CHARLES E. BOUCHARD, OP

Liguori
ONE LIGUORI DRIVE
LIGUORI MO 63057-9999

*Imprimi Potest:*
Harry Grile, CSsR, Provincial
Denver Province, The Redemptorists

*Imprimatur:* "In accordance with c. 827, permission to publish is granted on June 26, 2013, by Rev. Msgr. John F. Canary, Vicar General of the Archdiocese of Chicago. Permission to publish is an official declaration of ecclesiastical authority that the material is free from doctrinal and moral error. No legal responsibility is assumed by the granting of this permission."

Published by Liguori Publications
Liguori, Missouri 63057

To order, call 800-325-9521
www.liguori.org

**Cataloging-in-Publication Data is on file with the Library of Congress.**

p ISBN 978-0-7648-2484-5
e ISBN 978-0-7648-6933-4

Liguori Publications, a nonprofit corporation, is an apostolate of The Redemptorists. To learn more about The Redemptorists, visit Redemptorists.com.

Printed in the United States of America
18 17 16 15 14  /  5 4 3 2 1
First Edition

# Contents

## CHAPTER 3
### Questions About Marriage, Family, and Divorce    41

## CHAPTER 4
### Questions About Homosexuality
### and Sex Outside of Marriage    53

# CHAPTER 5
## Questions About Reproduction, Family Planning, and Abortion    **65**

## Conclusion

## Resources    **83**
## Endnotes    **87**

# Introduction

Sex is one of the most important human realities. Saint Thomas Aquinas ranks it right up there with food. The pleasures of taste and touch are fundamental joys in human life, but they also create the possibility of the most serious sins. We see this borne out today as we recognize the seriousness of addictive behavior. Just think about how hard it is to overcome addiction to food, alcohol, or drugs. The drive for satisfaction using these substances is powerful and difficult to control. The drive for sexual satisfaction is perhaps even more powerful because it engages our entire personalities. Perhaps because of its power and importance in our lives, sex gets a lot of attention, but not always in a good way. This is especially true in the Church, where many Catholics identify sex with sin, or simply with "no." This is unfortunate because our tradition has far more to say about sex than that.

Sex is holy; sex is a sacrament; sex is the way we participate in God's own creative act. Sex can also be violent, manipulative, and destructive. In fact, most serial killers are not killing just for the fun of it but because their sexual appetites have become seriously distorted toward violence rather than love and mutuality.

## Three misconceptions

There are three common misconceptions about sex that I shall try to address as I answer questions in *Sexuality and Morality*. The first is that sex is only about acts, or about what I *do*. The reality is that because sexuality exists prior to sexual activity, it is really concerned primarily with persons and with *who we are*. I might never have sex, but I am still a sexual person, a man or a woman who has a biological sex as well as a masculine or feminine sexuality. Acts, of course, are important, but they are secondary to my overall sexual personality. Sex is not just about what I do, but about who I am. This is why we will stress not just sexual sins, but sexual virtues and moral qualities that make well-rounded and happy persons.

The second misconception is that sexual sins are somehow worse than any other kind. Our society is very conflicted about this. On the one hand, we see all kinds of sexual activity on TV and in the movies. Much of it is casual and appears to be harmless or recreational. On the other hand, we have dozens of laws prohibiting sexual harassment, and we recoil in horror if a woman is raped or a child is sexually abused. Sexuality is a profound human power, and that is perhaps why the Church has historically devoted so much attention to it. But it is wrong to say that sexual sins are worse than others. Sins against justice, charity, and truth can be far worse and far more destructive. We need only think about the economic disparities in the world or the lies and hubris that lead to war to know that this is true.

The third misconception is that sex is just physical and therefore it has no lasting psychological or moral effects. It's true that we often portray sex as just sex, but adults know—and adolescents learn quickly enough—that sex can have enormous psychological and spiritual ramifications. Sex can have physical consequences like pregnancy or sexually transmitted diseases, but the most lasting effects of sex are often emotional.

## Three affirmations

Throughout this book my answers are formed by three main convictions that are rooted in the Catholic moral tradition.

The first is that we are sexual and that God wants us that way. God created us male and female, and we must consider that a great gift. God does not want us to repress, endure, or hide our sexuality. He wants us to claim who we are and live as good and faithful persons. We don't exist as persons in general; each one of us, even Jesus, is either male or female. The fact of Jesus' maleness is shocking to some. Could God not have become incarnate in some more inclusive, unisex manner rather than be limited to male or female? Yet the only way Jesus could be fully human is to be one gender or the other.

The second is that sex and sexuality are sacramental. This means that—like other good and authentic things we use in the seven sacraments (bread, wine, touch, water) to mediate God's grace—we ourselves as sexual persons are also sacraments. Think for a moment about the most wonderful *man* you know: someone who is just, holy, strong, caring, and generous. God's grace is mediated through the unique blend of masculine qualities he manifests. This man's life is sacramental.

Then think of a holy *woman*, someone who is equally just, holy, strong, caring, and generous. God also mediates his presence through her, but in a different way. The difference is sexuality. God is not present to us in general but through created things. Persons, sexual persons, are the first sacraments of God's presence. Most of what we know about God, we know through persons.

This extends further, into the physical aspect of sexuality. When a married couple experiences sexual intimacy, they are sacraments to one another. Every aspect of their married life—even the explicitly sexual—has the capacity to make grace present. In one of my favorite passages on marriage and sex, Denise Lardner Carmody actually draws a comparison between the sexual act and the life of the Trinity itself:

> When we make love, the love of Father, Son, and Spirit circulate, come into play....Can it be that the Spirit is the kindly light in which we are attractive to one another? Are the excitement, the arousal, the need, the pain we experience relevant to what makes up the life of God? Unless I am mistaken in my sense of the analogical character of Catholic theology, everything decent in our sexual loves bears the imprint of the united love that made us. Human orgasm bespeaks the ecstasy wrought by the divine perfection.[1]

The third affirmation is that morality and holiness are not just about obeying arbitrary laws. They are about wholeness, integration, happiness, and personal fulfillment. It comes as a surprise to many Catholics, but the moral life is fundamentally about finding happiness. This is not the superficial and transitory kind of happiness that we get when we buy a new motorcycle or win the lottery, but the deep, profound happiness that makes life worth living. Moral norms are important because they try to tell us what usually leads to human happiness and fulfillment, but in the end the moral life is a process of trial and error. In order to fully embrace these moral goods, we must first experience them.

As we get older, we learn more and more about how to achieve this kind of profound happiness and we become more skilled at actually achieving it. Bill Murray's movie *Groundhog Day* is an excellent example of this. In the movie, Murray's character experiences living the same day over and over again. At first he tries to manipulate things to his advantage, and then he realizes that there is something more, and he begins to think about how to really make things work—for the long run. Eventually, his selfish manipulation begins to give way to virtue.

Virtue requires that we learn to think for the long term and ask ourselves what will really be fulfilling to us, what will make us who God wants us to be. Holiness is not about becoming someone else, but about becoming fully who we are. No one says this better than Thomas Merton:

> The seeds that are planted in my liberty at every moment, by God's will, are the seeds of my own identity, my own reality, my own happiness, my own sanctity. *For me to be a saint means to be myself.* Therefore the problem of finding out who I am is discovering my true life. The secret of my identity is hidden in the love and mercy of God. Therefore there is only one problem on which all my existence, my peace and my happiness depend: to discover myself in discovering God....[2]

Even the saints were sexual. God's grace in their lives did not destroy that and replace it with something else. Grace brought it to perfection. As we explore all these very specific questions, let us keep that important lesson in mind.

The questions in this book are based on real questions posed by Catholics in a number of U.S. parishes. They reflect the questions that have come up in my own experience in spiritual direction and confession, and I believe they represent most of the concerns adult Catholics have about sex, morality, and spirituality. The answers are brief and the treatment is nonsystematic, but I hope they will be an invitation to take a closer look at the Church's tradition and resources.

# CHAPTER 1

# Love, Morality, and Sexuality

It has been said that we are all "co-creators" with God. This is true in our work, where we try to bring God's creation to completion. It is also true in political life where we cooperate with one another in order to achieve the common good on earth. To the extent that we do this, we actually foreshadow the reign of God.

One of the most powerful ways in which we co-create with God is in love and procreation. In marital love, persons are actually able to create life that is endowed with an eternal soul. Although there are many cases in which people enter into this process recklessly and without concern for consequences, it is one of the most serious things two human persons can do.

## A note on moral decision making

In addition to love and sexuality, we will also discuss morality in this chapter and those that follow. It may be important to define exactly what we mean by this word. Morality is a particular kind of knowing. It is not just knowing facts or knowing mathematical or scientific truth that results from rigorous reasoning. Nor is it knowing how to make something, as when an artist "knows" how to create a beautiful song or painting.

Moral knowing is practical knowing, or knowing what is to be done. It requires understanding of general principles and the ability to apply them to concrete situations. From an early age we learn to make moral decisions, and as we grow older we acquire a certain skill that comes with a well-formed conscience.

Conscience is both a general ability and a specific judgment; the *Catechism of the Catholic Church* describes conscience as "a judgment of reason whereby the human person recognizes the moral quality of a concrete act" that has been performed, is being performed, or will be performed in the future (*CCC* 1778). All of us have at least a minimal moral sense of right and wrong, but the complex choices that face us require that we train or form this moral sense. We call this "formation of conscience," a lifelong task that requires the ability to see the reality before us clearly and to make sound decisions based on reason, Scripture, Church teaching, advice from others, and openness to the guidance of the Holy Spirit.

Catholics frequently ask about the relationship between conscience and Church teaching as though we have to choose one or the other. I have heard people say, "Either I follow Church teaching or I follow my conscience." In fact there is a delicate balance between the Church's moral teaching, which is rooted in Scripture and sifted through centuries of human experience, and the autonomy of conscience. The two are not in opposition. Conscience is an ability or skill that uses Church teaching in order to arrive at a concrete moral decision, here and now. Conscience is the only way in which we can see the moral world before us. Like a lens, it may be cloudy or cracked, but it is still essential to moral discernment.

The *Catechism* tells us we "must always obey the certain judgment of...conscience" (*CCC* 1790), but it is important to note that for a conscientious decision to be both correct and certain, it must flow from a conscience that is well-formed and sincere in its search for the right answer. This sincere search for moral truth is the most difficult part of moral maturity. We can take the easy way out and choose the most convenient thing or the thing that gives us the most short-term pleasure. But a sincere search means we really want to know what is right, what is *really* fulfilling, even if it is difficult to carry out in practice.

Moral carelessness or deliberate failure to inform ourselves to the fullest extent possible makes us liable to sin. In sexual matters, the drive for satisfaction and sexual pleasure can be so strong that it causes us to rationalize or take moral shortcuts in order to deceive ourselves into making the wrong decision.

No one chooses evil for its own sake. We only choose a good, even if it is only an apparent good or a very short-term good. In sexual ethics, the good we choose is usually pleasure (although it could be money, influence, or prestige). While none of these things is bad, the choice of them becomes sinful if in choosing them we reject a greater or more lasting good. So the spouse who has an affair chooses the affection and pleasure that the affair provides but rejects the far more important good of fidelity and trust.

Throughout this book we will refer to virtue and virtuous choices. Virtue is the moral skill or quality of character that comes from repeated good choices. This makes it clear that morality is not just a matter of doing the right thing but also of becoming the type of person who does the good thing readily and happily.

Virtue is much like musical or athletic skill that begins with basic talent that is trained to respond in the best possible way. This is why an accomplished musician is sometimes referred to as a "virtuoso." Through training her ability, the musician is able to produce something beautiful with no apparent effort. The skill has become second nature: It pleases others, and it also creates joy in the musician.

In a similar way, we acquire virtue gradually as we practice by making various moral choices. Eventually our virtue, or inclination to do the right thing, becomes stronger; then it begins to influence future choices. The truly virtuous person not only achieves morally beautiful acts but finds fulfillment and happiness in doing so.

### How does the Church define "love?"

Love is a word with many different meanings. We can talk about God's love for us, or about our love for our mothers, or our love for chocolate or skiing. Greek philosophy distinguishes between *philia,* or brotherly love, and *eros,* or sexual love. The questions in this book relate primarily to *eros,* or the kind of love that is involved in romantic attraction and marriage, but they also speak of a broader kind of love that sustains the families and societies in which marriage takes place.

Sexual love has two aspects. The first is familiar. It's reflected in the song "It's So Easy (to Fall in Love)" made famous by Buddy Holly and redone by Linda Ronstadt. There's a lot of truth to this title; it signals the attraction that leads to love. Everyone's had the experience of being smitten by someone, experiencing love at first sight. This person is someone I desire, someone I want, someone who really pushes all my buttons. That's the "fall" part.

But love is not all attraction. It also requires commitment. To love someone in the deepest sense means to constantly will the best for that person. After the attraction, we continue to love this person for who he or she is, not just for the physical satisfaction or comfort he or she gives us. Attraction comes naturally, but then we have to make the love real by a deliberate choice to love this person "for better or worse," as the wedding vows say. It's easy to say "we're in love" when sexual attraction exerts its power, but what we're often experiencing is love of the sexual thrill rather than love of the person. It's not that the two things can't go together, but unfortunately they often don't. It's easy to say "I love you" for a single night, harder to say "I love you" over a period of five, ten, or fifty years. That is the work of a lifetime.

For Christians, love has yet another aspect. We enjoy the physical attraction and the possibilities it holds; we may love the person through a commitment. But as Christians, we also love as God loves us, without counting the cost and without hesitation. In short, we must love out of an act of faith, binding ourselves to that other person and his or her destiny just as God bound himself to us. In real love we constantly will the best for the person we love; we must also be ready to pay the cost that comes with it. When we love someone as God loves us and because God loved us first, our love becomes sacramental.

As Pope Benedict XVI notes in his encyclical God Is Love, sexual, charitable, and community love cannot ultimately be separated. We grow into them as grace perfects them within us. The Pope writes:

> *Eros* and *agape*—ascending love and descending love—can never be completely separated. The more the two, in their different aspects, find a proper unity in the one reality of love, the more the true nature of love in general is realized. Even if *eros* is at first mainly covetous and ascending, a fascination for the great promise of happiness, in drawing near to the other, it is less and less concerned with itself, increasingly seeks the happiness of the other, is concerned more and more with the beloved, bestows itself and wants to "be there for" the other.

Speaking to a group of young Italians in Umbria in 2013, Pope Francis said that the love we find in marriage is risky, but it is a risk worth taking. "Jesus did not save us provisionally," the Pope said, "he saved us definitively." Therefore, our love should not be provisional either. We must be willing to take the risk of committing ourselves permanently, making marriage a vocation rather than a steppingstone.

## What do we mean by sexuality?

Sexuality is perhaps the most complex and mysterious aspect of human experience. We can talk about sex and think we understand it. Most persons are easily categorized as male or female on the basis of certain genetic markers and external characteristics that are easily observable.

Sexuality, however, has a number of different meanings and is not so easily characterized. In one sense, sexuality is our objective sexual identity, the mix of genetics, psychology, roles, gender, and attitudes that make us who we are. Sexuality is more than just male or female—it begins with biological sex but encompasses a whole range of experiences and attractions. God has created us with a specific identity or personality. Each of us has a distinctive sexual personality, one that is unique to us and not quite like that of anyone else. Yet the exact nature of this identity is not fully knowable, even to ourselves. It is only in the next life, when God brings us to completion, that who we really are will be fully known to us.

Sexuality is pervasive because it is only through the lens of our sexuality that we can experience the world or engage in relationships with others. We can't relate to people in general but only through our unique sexual makeup. This is true even for celibates. Even though they may not have sex, they still are sexual persons who have a distinct experience of the world because they are male or female.

Whether I am engaged in an intimate conversation with my best friend or receiving change from the toll collector on the turnpike, I am doing so as a sexual person. Sometimes this is more obvious, for instance when we are doing typically women's things with women or typically male things with other men, but whatever the context, we experience everything through our unique sexual perspective.

The second way in which we experience our sexuality is through genital expression. If I have sex with someone, I am engaging in a specific and privileged type of bodily communication that engages me at a profound level. The person to whom I am attracted is determined by a specific pattern of attraction that has been described as a "love map." So some women are attracted to tall, lanky, blond men; others to stocky men with curly black hair. Similarly, some men might find short brunettes most appealing, while others are invariably attracted to women with red hair and green eyes. Even though many factors ultimately determine with whom we eventually fall in love, these initial physical attractions are rooted in our sexuality.

## What does the Bible say about sex and sexuality?

The Bible is a collection of books that was written over many centuries. It would be impossible to even begin to relate what the Bible says about sex. However, among the hundreds of references to sex and sexuality in the Bible, there are three or four that are particularly important and that must control the way in which we understand the rest of them.

- *Creation* (Genesis 1:27–28). The first creation account says, "God created mankind in his image; in the image of God he created them; male and female he created them. God blessed them and God said to them: Be fertile and multiply; fill the earth and subdue it." From the start, sexuality was a share in God's creative act. The second account (Genesis 2:23–25) speaks of Eve's being created as "bone of my bones and flesh of my flesh" and affirms the sanctity of marriage by saying this is why a man leaves his father and his mother and "clings to his wife, and the two of them become one body." Again and again in the Hebrew Scriptures, God uses sex and procreation to further not only the act of creation but God's own salvific purpose.

- *Sin of Adam and Eve* (Genesis 3). Original sin did not ruin sexuality, but it sure did take some of the joy out of it! We inherit Adam and Eve's sin as a very stubborn tendency to do the wrong thing. As St. Paul said, "I do not do the good I want, but I do the evil I do not want" (Romans 7:19). The sin of Adam and Eve reminds us that in sex, as well as in all other areas of our lives, moral goodness no longer comes naturally. We need persistence and grace to grow in virtue and lead holy lives.

- *The woman caught in adultery* (John 7:53—8:11) *and the woman at the well* (John 4:3–30). These stories are both gripping and tense. In both cases, Jesus encounters a woman who is not only an outsider but a sinner. We might expect that Jesus would condemn them or distance himself from them, but he does not. In fact, he even violates social conventions when he asks the Samaritan woman for a drink from the well. She in turn understands who he is and runs off to proclaim him as Lord. These two stories are powerful accounts of forgiveness and redemption. They remind us that sexual sins are no worse than others. Forgiveness is available to anyone through faith.

- *Love your wives as Christ loves the Church* (Ephesians 5). In this passage, St. Paul exhorts husbands and wives to love one another just as Christ loves the Church. Although we sometimes get distracted by Paul's admonition that wives should be "subject to their husbands," the real import of this passage is that Paul elevates marriage and physical love to the level of God's own love for us. This passage also suggests that marriage is a reflection of God's own covenant with us, a covenant through which he offers us salvation. Reflecting the understanding of covenant in the Jewish Scriptures, St. Paul portrays Christ's relationship to the Church as a marriage: loving, fruitful, and eternal.

## Is sexual morality the same as other kinds of morality, or are there different rules?

Sexual morality obviously differs from other kinds of morality because it deals with different aspects of human life. The moral questions we face in business ethics, for example, are not the same as those about marriage, family, and procreation. Still, the goal or purpose of all morality is human happiness—and that ranges across all the moral questions in our lives. What's more, we are called to wholeness. We cannot achieve happiness when we are fragmented and divided. In that sense, the rules for sexual morality are part of a much larger framework that encompasses the whole person. If to be fully human involves being just, truthful, respectful, generous, and productive, we can see ways in which these values play out in sexual ethics, business ethics, or even environmental ethics.

Pope Francis caused a big stir when, not long after his election, he said the Church should not be obsessed with certain moral issues to the exclusion of others. When he said this he was not discounting the importance of certain high-profile moral issues. Rather, he was saying we have to constantly move to great wholeness and to appreciation of the "big picture" of human life. "When we speak about these issues," he said, "we have to talk about them in a context." That context is the whole narrative of human life. Jesus came not to save just parts of us. He came to save our entire selves—social, sexual, economic, and political. Morality is not just about sex or abortion. It is about becoming whole and holy.[3]

Consider the virtue of justice. When we think of justice, we might be more inclined to think it is the virtue of business people, politicians, or lawyers. We would not readily associate it with sexual morality. Yet many of the most serious sexual sins are actually sins against justice. The woman who commits adultery is committing a serious injustice against her husband, her children, and perhaps against her accomplice's wife. The moral question about divorce includes justice, too. When we marry someone, we make a public commitment to another person. We are bound in justice to honor that commitment. If we marry in the Church, that commitment is made in the name of the Trinity, so that we owe fidelity not only to our spouse and to our community of friends, but also to God. Justice is central to morality, even sexual morality. In fact, it has been said that the only true sexual sins are those against justice. William E. May describes the relationship:

> There is a deep connection between sexual morality and social justice. Justice requires that we give to everyone what is his or her due. This means recognizing every human being for what a human being is: a precious, irreplaceable,

nonsubstitutable person. Sexual coition by the unmarried violates justice as well as chastity, because in such coition the priceless worth of the person is not recognized.[4]

Temperance provides us with another example of a virtue that encompasses many different aspects of life. We usually think of temperance as relating to food and drink, but it is actually the virtue that controls our desire for any satisfying thing—food, drink, and sex, to be sure, but also anger and retribution. Temperance does not mean eliminating desire for good things but rather training it so that it operates in our best interests.

So with regard to food, we may develop the virtue of temperate eating or drinking—not too much, not too little. Or we may seek temperance in speech so we avoid the satisfaction of gossip, anger, or vengeance. Or we may become sexually temperate so we value and revere sexual pleasure and attraction, but we seek it in moderation and always in the context of respect for other persons. We call this kind of temperance *chastity.*

Temperance even plays out in the business world. Here it can mean resisting the temptation to make too much money, own too many things, or control too many companies. The temperate business person is, like the temperate husband or wife, someone who seeks gratification and success while respecting persons.

Because morality leads us to wholeness, the same virtues guide our behavior in many different aspects of life. This is also why we say that a person who truly has one virtue has them all. If they truly lack one of the virtues, they lack all of them. This is a way of describing the unity of the person.

## No one seems to talk about mortal and venial sin any more. Do we still think there is a difference?

Catholics of a certain age remember well the difference between mortal and venial sin. When the practice of frequent confession declined, we didn't talk about these two kinds of sin as much, but there are still some important differences between them.

16

A mortal sin, as its name suggests, is a serious or "deadly sin." Venial sins are less serious. We can judge the seriousness of a sin in two ways. The first is based on the matter of the sin, or what I actually did; for example, it is obviously a more serious matter to defraud an investor or assault a spouse than it is to tell a lie about how fast I was going when I got stopped for speeding. This is an objective determination of the sinfulness of an act. Some things by their nature are worse than others.

A second way to assess sin is from a subjective perspective so that the intention is more important than the act in itself. Even if the act itself is relatively minor, it can be a mortal sin depending on why I do it. For instance, I might fail to lock the front door of a friend's house, which is not a serious sin in itself. It becomes serious if my intention in failing to lock the door is to leave the home open to burglary by an accomplice.

On the other hand, I might do something objectively serious (like, betray an important confidence); but if I do it under coercion or without full understanding, my own personal moral culpability might actually be quite limited; the matter is mortal, but my own sin or moral responsibility is venial. Confessors often have to sort out the matter from the intention. It is not just what I do, but my freedom, understanding, and purpose in doing it.

**I have not been to confession in years. How do I start?**

First, it's a very good idea to forget about childhood experiences of confession, especially if they were painful or unpleasant. We don't dress, eat, recreate, or talk as we did when we were children. Similarly, we set aside our childhood approaches to morality and confession in favor of a more adult approach.

There are two big differences between childhood and adult experiences of the moral life. The first is that, for adults, the moral life is not just a list of do's and don'ts. For adults the questions are not just, "What did I do wrong?" but rather, "Where did I fail to do what I know I should have done?" As adults we should be more concerned with patterns and habits than with individual acts. These patterns and habits are what we refer to as virtues and vices. While children don't usually have the experience to have developed either, adults do. As we grow older, we should be focusing on the big picture by asking ourselves, "Where is my life going? If I am not on the right path, how can I get there?" Morality for adults is more focused on who I am than just on what I have done.

Second, even if confession is less frequent than it was when you were a child, it should be much more serious and should be done face-to-face with a priest rather than during a few short moments in a confessional. If you have not been to confession for some time, make an appointment with a priest and plan to have a serious adult conversation about where you have succeeded, where you have failed, and how you can take serious steps toward conversion. Confession is not just about getting dressed down for your failings. It is also about acknowledging moments of grace in your life and opening your heart to God's renewing presence through forgiveness and penance.

## Is there a sexual sin that God won't forgive?

No. We have already noted that sometimes people think that sexual sins are worse than others, but this is a result of cultural attitudes toward sex that make it seem shameful or dishonorable. If we see sexuality as God's gift, then it is hard to imagine that sexual sins are, by their very nature, worse than sins against justice or compassion. With repentance and determination not to commit the sin again, God's forgiveness is always available.

This is not to understate the difficulty of discussing, let alone confessing, our sexual sins. Sometimes we feel our darkest secrets concern sexual sins and we think, "If anyone ever knew what I did they would think I'm a terrible person." This is rarely the case, however, and usually our fears about our failures in chastity are far worse than the reality.

As a young priest, the first year I was ordained I was invited to hear confessions on Good Friday and Holy Saturday. I accepted the invitation from the pastor, eager to get some experience in real priestly ministry. I was in the confessional for several hours each day, and I can honestly say that I have never heard anything of a sexual nature that I didn't hear in those two days. There are exotic and bizarre sexual sins, to be sure, but most of us are guilty of the garden variety. We should never hesitate to take them to the sacrament of reconciliation.

It is also important (for confessors and penitents alike) to remember that serious and chronic sexual sin can often involve the possibility of addiction that requires psychological intervention as well as spiritual care. I will address this at more length in a later question.

### What does the Church know about sex? All its leaders are celibate men.

First of all, not all priests were always celibate; in fact, some were even married and had children prior to their ordination as priests. Second, priests may be celibate, but we aren't neuter! I noted above that even though not everyone has sex, everyone is sexual and has sexuality. Even celibates are sexual persons who have desires, attractions and, yes, sexual sins to confess.

In the past, it was common for seminaries essentially to ask students to "check their sexuality at the door" when beginning studies for the priesthood. Unfortunately, this attitude of denial and repression sometimes fostered emotional immaturity and may even have contributed to sickness that led to sexual abuse of minors. Seminary education has changed dramatically in the past generation or so. Today seminary formation is concerned not just with academics but with human, spiritual, and ministerial formation. This means that the first things we look for in considering candidates for the priesthood are emotional and sexual wholeness. We do not accept candidates whose histories reflect inordinate or inappropriate sexual activity, nor do we accept those who refuse to admit they have sexuality. We are looking for men who have a healthy appreciation for their own sexuality and who are able to speak honestly about their emotions and needs.

Celibacy and married life have more in common than one might think. Both are concerned with renunciation and self sacrifice; both require a balance between affection and work. And both require a spiritual life nourished by prayer, Scripture, and solid friendships. So even though celibates may not have had genital sexual experience, they should have a profound awareness of the human goods and values that underlie every human relationship.

Priests are sometimes referred to as "physicians of the soul" or as "spiritual doctors." They see a lot of "patients," and have an enormous store of knowledge about what constitutes holiness and sin. Just as an excellent physician does not necessarily have to have cancer in order to treat it, so a good priest can provide sound advice to married couples even though he himself has never been married.

### I am disgusted and embarrassed that so many priests have molested children. How can this happen?

The clergy sexual-abuse crisis has indeed been a tragedy and an embarrassment—not just for Catholic lay people but for clergy as well. Sexual abuse—bad enough in itself—was compounded when parental and family trust were betrayed by misconduct.

Because of the complexity of sexuality and sexual attraction, it is difficult to say why some people develop an attraction to children. Indeed, there are at least two distinct kinds of pedophilia. True pedophilia involves attraction to prepubescent children. It is deep-rooted and difficult to treat. Attraction to postpubescent children—boys or girls—is different. Unlike true pedophilia, it can admit of a certain amount of mutuality, and in some cases (for example, a seventeen-year-old boy and a sixteen-year-old girl) the lines between acceptable and unacceptable are somewhat blurred.

Allegations against priests include both kinds of sexual abuse, although by far the largest number involved adolescents. In a study commissioned by the U.S. Conference of Catholic Bishops in 2002, the John Jay College of Criminal Justice found that between 1950 and 2002 there were a total of 5,349 allegations of abuse made against priests or deacons. Ninety percent of the dioceses and 60 percent of religious orders surveyed reported allegations. Of all priests active during those years, between 2.5 percent and 7 percent of diocesan priests had allegations made against them, and 1 percent to 3 percent of religious priests. It does not appear that the incidence of sexual abuse among the clergy is higher than among the population at large.

For priests, sexual abuse may be rooted in their own early childhood, in a family history of sexual abuse, or in a kind of adolescent fixation that may have resulted partly from seminary formation programs that discouraged or punished healthy peer relationships. Such priests may never have actually grown up emotionally. They continued to relate to adolescents or teenagers well into their own adulthood. A.W. Richard Sipe, who has written widely on how to achieve true celibacy, notes the impact of early childhood experiences and the importance of keeping them out in the open:

> Early sexual impressions and experiences have lifelong effects. The memory traces laid down are the emotional and psychic raw material of later development. They are best remembered and absorbed rather than repressed or forgotten, because experience will have its effects—the more conscious, the more usable and invaluable.[5]

Unfortunately, sexual abuse is not limited to the clergy. Although exact numbers are difficult to obtain, we know that sexual abuse is widespread throughout society. The USCCB study cited available statistics that show about 27 percent of women and 16 percent of men report a history of sexual abuse, but only 5 percent of these incidents were reported to the police. Twenty-six percent of the incidents had never been reported to anyone prior to the study. While the media have drawn attention to clerical abuse, it has largely ignored the reality of family-sexual abuse by parents, relatives, and family friends.

# CHAPTER 2
# Sexual Practices in Today's Culture

In the United States during the first half of the twentieth century, sexual morality was clear and consistent for most people, and especially for Catholics. There was a general consensus that premarital and extramarital sex, homosexual activity, and out-of-wedlock children were morally unacceptable. By the mid-1960s, however, two events changed everything.

The first was the appearance of the pill, oral contraceptives that made it possible for women to avoid pregnancy easily and secretly. The second thing was the commission convened by Pope Paul VI in 1963 to reexamine the Church's long-standing ban on artificial contraceptives. He did this after the Anglican Church had considered a similar policy and decided to reverse it.

Ultimately Pope Paul decided to uphold the Church's tradition and not allow the use of the pill or other artificial contraceptives. However, for many Catholics the very fact that the issue had been raised seemed to give permission to start giving other points of view about contraception the same weight as Church teaching.

These ecclesial events were just the tip of the cultural iceberg. Around the globe, the 1960s were years of intense and rapid cultural change of the kind that occurs in regular cycles through history. It is hard to know exactly what caused the sexual revolution of the sixties, but no doubt the Kinsey Reports on human sexuality, the availability and effectiveness of the pill and of antibiotics that could treat sexually transmitted diseases, and the prosperity and mobility that followed World War II and women's "liberation" from the prevailing model of domestic life had something to do with it. Whatever the causes, the effects of this revolution changed sexual attitudes dramatically. Our knowledge of human sexuality and sexual practices expanded exponentially, and we became much more comfortable talking about sex. Many of the questions we will address would never have been asked, let alone answered, in a Catholic book prior to the 1960s!

## Is it possible to cultivate strong moral values in a culture saturated with media images of marital infidelity and sex outside of marriage?

The debate about whether TV violence causes violent behavior has raged for years, but according to the American Psychiatric Association, "the debate is over." In a web statement, "Psychiatric Effects of Media Violence," the APA says, "Over the last three decades, the one overriding finding in research on the mass media is that exposure to media portrayals of violence increases aggressive behavior in children."

Sex is at least as prevalent on TV as violence, and sex is often presented as a casual activity without risk or consequences. Evidence is mounting that it also affects the behavior of young people. Two studies by the Rand Corporation[6] found that:

- Teens who watch a lot of television with sexual content are twice as likely to initiate intercourse in the following year.

- Television shows in which characters *talk* about sex affect teens just as much as programs that actually show sexual activity.

This means first of all that parents should be aware of what their children, especially preteens, are watching. This might mean watching the shows your kids watch with *their* eyes. Parents might ask themselves, "What conclusions would I draw from the behavior portrayed in this show if I were thirteen?"

Second, parents should be sure that their children have adequate doctrinal and spiritual formation so they are able to exercise some critical judgment about the behavior they see portrayed on television. Some Catholics resist explicit sexual education for fear that it would introduce children to the possibility of sexual activity too early. Yet unless your children watch no television at all, they are likely being introduced to detailed information about sexual behavior at an early age. Parents should assume that children are seeing and absorbing information about sex, and that their consciences are probably not formed adequately.

The good news from the Rand study is that even though children are affected by the sex they see on TV, they can also learn from shows that realistically portray the risk of casual sex. "The researchers concluded that entertainment shows that include portrayal of sexual risks and consequences can potentially have two beneficial effects: They can teach accurate messages about sexual risks and they can stimulate a conversation with adults that can reinforce those messages."

The Rand study was mostly concerned about health risks associated with sexual activity, and that is a start. But there are also significant moral risks that accompany casual sex. Even if they send their children to Catholic schools, parents still have the first responsibility for the moral formation of their children. Sexually explicit TV shows can provide a perfect opportunity for parents to begin an informal catechetical session with their children on sexual morality by asking, "Well, what did you think of that?" Parents might also think about making up a list of moral values (such as fidelity, truthfulness, respect, and wholeness) and referring to them whenever the occasion presents itself. This might help children see that morality is not just obeying rules but finding creative ways to realize moral values and become better persons in the decisions they make.

## What does it mean to go "too far?"

First of all, let's make it clear that we are talking here about pre-marital sex. Presumably married couples can make their own decisions about how far is too far.

Our moral tradition rests on the principle that any "directly willed sexual pleasure outside of marriage" is a mortal sin. There are two reasons why we say this. The first is that, as we all know, "one thing leads to another." Emotions being what they are, we can easily get in over our heads and say with our bodies far more than we mean to. Another way to talk about this is to say that affection should be proportionate in intensity to the level and depth of the relationship. This means that intense and intimate sexual sharing should be reserved to marriage because it is only in a committed relationship that we can risk exposing ourselves in all our vulnerability to another person. Since emotions and sexual arousal are spontaneous and often not directly willed or intended, we must also be sure that we are *deciding* to express our affection in this way rather than being dragged into it by unruly emotions.

### The *Catechism of the Catholic Church* says we are all called to be chaste. How can I be chaste if I am married?

The *Catechism* does indeed say that all the baptized—not just celibates—are called to chastity (see CCC 2337). It describes chastity as "the successful integration of sexuality within the person and thus the inner unity of [a person] in his bodily and spiritual being." This does not mean the same thing for everyone. For married persons, chastity does not mean no sex; rather, it means using your sexual ability generously and in a way that makes you and your spouse more whole. Marriage marked by abusive sex, cheating, sexual fantasies, and/or masturbation lacks chastity.

Chastity is a virtue, a moral skill that is marked by the ability to relate to another person as a whole person, without deceit, manipulation, and self-will. Chaste persons live integrated lives so that their will, their desire, their knowledge all work together toward the good of the person. Chastity resists fragmentation and compartmentalization. This is how the *Catechism* further describes it:

> Sexuality, in which man's belonging to the bodily and biological world is expressed, becomes personal and truly human when it is integrated into the relationship of one person to another, in the complete and lifelong mutual gift of a man and a woman (*CCC* 2337).

For celibates, chastity involves a renunciation of sexual activity—not because it is bad or sinful, but because they have chosen to direct their sexual energies to a kind of generativeness that does not involve exclusive relationships, genital sex, or childbearing. Celibacy and chastity do not necessarily go together, however. A man who has been perfectly celibate his whole life could still lack the virtue of chastity if he is continually conflicted, plagued with sexual temptations, and resentful of having given up the possibility of sexual satisfaction. As a virtue, chastity must be marked not only by purity of mind and body but of heart, through willingness and joy.

No one acquires the virtue of chastity entirely on his own. To a large extent, chastity depends on the quality of our friendships. Author Paul J. Wadell once said that friendships are "schools for virtue." He cites a number of reasons why friendship is essential to the moral life:

> First, good friendships form important virtues and qualities of character such as caring, generosity, patience, thoughtfulness, kindness, sympathy and forgiveness. It is through good and lasting friendships that we grow morally, develop our characters and acquire essential virtues....Second, friendships...draw us out of ourselves and teach us to care

for others for their own sake. A fundamental activity of every friendship is seeking the good of the friend....Friendships call us out of ourselves and challenge us to see beyond the pinched horizons of self-concern and self-interest...the life of any true friendship works against this narrowing by summoning us to invest in another's good and to remain devoted to her best interest even when doing so requires sacrifice from us.[7]

This is particularly true for chastity. Whether in celibacy or in marriage, the virtue of chastity is nurtured by friendships that are marked by honesty, reciprocity, and challenge. In marriage, this "virtue friend" will usually be our spouse; but even celibates need close friendships that draw the best out of them and keep them honest and whole.

## Is sexuality an expression of love or a tool for procreation?

In a word, it's both. There was a time when the Church spoke about the "primacy of the procreative intent," meaning that every sexual act had to be primarily for the purpose of procreation. In recent years, however, procreation and mutual love have been established as equally important. Sexual acts must be open to the possibility of procreation *and* they must also be authentic expressions of committed love between two persons. It is not quite accurate to say that procreation is only a tool, since that implies that it is just a means to an end, like a mechanic would use various tools in order to fix my car. In marriage, the sexual act is not just a means to an end; it is both the love itself and possibility of new life. It is a beautiful, valuable thing in itself, *and* it is an occasion for procreation.

One way of describing marital sexuality is to say that sex is a language, an intimate self-speaking to another person. We acquire our sexual language gradually, from the time we are children, just like we acquire verbal and written language. Initially our vocabulary is limited, and our attempts to speak are full of errors and partial sentences. As we mature, we learn to speak in full, grammatically correct, and even elegant sentences. With sex, we start with a small sexual vocabulary and gradually learn to speak more fully and effectively.

Like any other language, sex can be used to say many things. It can be used manipulatively, deceitfully, or vengefully. It can also be used to speak love, care, and trust. Because this sexual language develops gradually, it can also become distorted or impeded. Traumatic events in childhood can lead to stilted or pathological sexuality. This is why adults who have been sexually abused as children may find it difficult to establish long-term and rewarding relationships in marriage. It also explains how children who were punished or abused for having sexual thoughts or playing sexually with other children may develop deviant sexual practices in adulthood. Experts say that the violence of abuse trespasses into their sexual development and takes root. It also explains why sexual abuse often passes from one generation to another. It is partly the result of learned behavior by children at a time when their own sexuality is malleable and open to outside influences. This is why sex education for children has to take place in an environment of trust, honesty, candor, and compassion.

## Is masturbation still a sin?

While Woody Allen once said that masturbation was "sex with someone I love," it should be clear from what we have said already that sex is essentially a social activity; it is inherently addressed to a person to whom we have made a commitment in marriage.

Solitary sexual activity is devoid of procreative potential and lacks the mutuality that God intended. It has no value as a sign of love of commitment. Also, the sexual fantasies that accompany solitary sex are based upon objectifying a person, making the idea of a person merely instrumental to my own satisfaction. While it might be argued that these persons are indeed only fantasies, not real persons, in some cases there are connections between habitual, compulsive masturbation and the inability to establish normal relationships.

So yes, masturbation is still a sin because it falls far short of the goodness that we can achieve through our sexuality. However it is important to emphasize that not all instances of solitary sex are equally serious. The use of solitary sex to avoid marital relations or to punish a spouse is probably the most serious; sexual experimentation by teenagers when it is part of a transition to adulthood may lack full freedom and understanding and therefore would be judged far less harshly.

## If we have oral sex, are we still technically virgins?

There is a lot of chatter online about the morality of oral sex. I have the distinct impression that today there is a new casuistry that allows sexual gratification as long as it doesn't involve both sets of genitals. (I came across a website that asked, "Is oral sex the new good-night kiss?") In some cases, I fear that oral sex is allowed as sort of a down payment on a committed relationship, to keep a partner interested without really making a commitment. It is used to indicate serious attraction but not real self-giving. Oral sex outside of marriage is a compartmentalized, inhuman kind of sexual sharing. It leads to giving one organ of your body, but not yourself.

If you engage in oral sex, you may be a virgin technically, but you are not a virgin in any meaningful moral sense. Sexual intimacy that leads to climax is sex, no matter what you call it.

## In our society, is virginity still a desirable thing?

The important thing about virginity is integrity. "Holiness" is in many ways equivalent to "wholeness," and being whole is really the goal of the moral life. This means I should strive for that wholeness as much as possible. If I engage in sex, at least physically, I am offering myself entirely to another person. Integrity demands that the rest of my personality—my heart, my soul, my emotions—go with my body. When I do otherwise, when I engage in sex with someone I do not really love, then I am essentially sacrificing my wholeness and integrity for immediate gratification.

If I choose to do this, I pay a heavy price: I either fragment myself more and more, or I have to protect parts of myself I do not want to share, compartmentalizing them and giving one part of myself to this person, one part to another person, and so on. It is easy to see how this can lead to a "dis-integrated person." So while physical virginity may be no big deal in *itself,* it is a powerful symbol of my wholeness and integrity as a person. I keep myself "intact" so that I can offer my *entire* self to the person I really love.

It may not have occurred to the person who wrote this question, but virginity can also be a vocation. There are persons, both male and female, who have made a very conscious decision to forego sex permanently in order to offer themselves as fully as possible to God. Some women choose consecrated virginity and live in convents with others who have made the same choice. They profess their vow of virginity publicly in a special rite that resembles the rite of ordination to the priesthood. Others live in the world as single, celibate adults. They do so as a personal act of faith, in imitation of Christ, and also as a sign to the world of singleness of purpose and integrity of life. Persons who make these courageous choices remind us that even in a sex-saturated culture, human fulfillment can be found in abstinence.

### Is the phenomenon of "hooking up" as a replacement for dating here to stay?

Until recently, I thought "hooking up" was something you hired a plumber to do. Fortunately, columnist Charles Blow of *The New York Times* set me straight. As a service to those of us over thirty, he defines it as follows: "Hooking up is a casual sexual encounter with no expectation of future emotional commitment. Think of it as a one-night stand with someone you know." Before writing a column on the topic, Mr. Blow called Kathleen Bogle, author of *Hooking Up: Sex, Dating and Relationships on Campus.* What he found out was that for some young people today, everything seemed to be exactly the opposite of what he remembered. "Under the old model, you dated a few times and, if you really liked the person, you might consider having sex. Under the new model, you hook up a few times and, if you really like the person, you might consider going on a date."[8]

Bogle's study was focused on what is actually happening on our campuses today. She wasn't interested in making any moral judgments. Others, including Laurie Fendrich, don't think it matters whether we make moral judgments about it or not. "I don't see any value in agonizing over the morality of hooking up," she says. "Once sexual morals have experienced a sea change the likes of hooking up, indignation is rather pointless. Besides, in some ways the demise of dating (and its predecessor, courtship) is a good thing. In a post-romantic age, where deep yearning is almost always the subject of irony, romantic courtship of any kind is almost quaint."[9]

We might hope that the climate on Catholic college campuses is better, but there is evidence that it is not. College theology professor Vigen Guroian recently suggested that his daughter's Catholic dormitory was not much better than a brothel. Colleges no longer stand *in loco parentis,* preferring instead to stand by while the lives and integrity of their students are ruined. Guroian writes of one Catholic college: "It fosters not growth into wholeness but the dissolution of personality, not the integration of learning and everyday living but their radical bifurcation. It most certainly does not support the Church's values of marriage and family."[10]

Hooking up presents a serious challenge to Catholic sexual ethics. It is the antithesis of an ethic based on commitment and permanence. It is based on the premise that the physical can be separated from the psychological, emotional, and spiritual. Its prevalence suggests a dramatic shift in our vision of sex and of the human person. Still, I am not quite ready to throw in the towel. The sexual revolution has continued to roll along since even before I was in college, but our ethic is not just an arbitrary set of rules. It is based on values like integrity, wholeness, and belief in the unity of body and soul that are real and tangible. I am confident that with help, young people will be able to experience these values—or at least the absence of them—and make appropriate changes in their beliefs and behavior.

### Is it always wrong to use pornography, even if you're married?

There are two problems with pornography. One is that it objectifies people. The other is that it objectifies people. I mean this to be emphatic, but I also say this because pornography is objectifying in at least two ways.

First, regardless of how or where it is used, pornography by its nature is making a person a means to an end: This photograph or movie is only instrumental to my own satisfaction. The damage is less, I suppose, when the person willingly submits to being photographed, but as an occupation it still seems to have very limited potential for enhancing personal dignity. When I buy or view pornography, I am cooperating with the process of human diminishment that produced it. In his book *Refusing to be a Man: Essays on Sex and Justice,* John Stoltenberg describes how the use of pornography makes us complicit in this objectification:

> Each consumer, each purchaser of a reproduced documentation of the original sexual objectification is complicitous in the commerce, a link in the chain of profit and hence he bears some responsibility, however widely shared by others, for the act of sexual objectification that took place in front of the camera to begin with....The act was not done *by* him, but as soon as he buys a documentation of it he becomes someone it was done *for,* someone whose intent—along

with that of many others—was collectively expressed and acted out in the original, particular act.[11]

Second, within marriage the problem is compounded because there is always a risk that in using pornography to improve marital sex, the pornography becomes an end rather than a means. It can become a substitute for the person I've married. Is the primary object of my love the person to whom I am married, or am I really making love to my fantasy, with a little help from my spouse? It is also possible that the pornography is important to one partner and unimportant or even repulsive to the other. Married couples who regularly use pornography need to have a long and candid talk about what this actually means to their relationship.

The objectification that characterizes pornography appears to be a greater problem for men than for women. In fact, John Stoltenberg says that this objectified view of sex is "considered the norm of male sexuality...and [as] a 'natural' and 'healthy' way of looking at other people." He raises disturbing questions about this male experience:

> What does it mean that a man's most routine, most repeated, most reliable, perhaps even most intensely "personal" erotic experiences are those that happen in relation to things, to bodies perceived and regarded as things, to images depicting bodies as things, to memories of images of bodies as things? What does it mean that he responds sexually to bodies as things and images of bodies as things in a way that is more or less constant, no matter whether another human being is actually with him?[12]

Stoltenberg's analysis makes it clear why pornography (and the solitary sex that often accompanies it) is both an injustice and a violation of our own human dignity.

## Is it wrong to call "800" sex numbers or to go to websites that promote sexual fantasy?

"800" numbers and sexually oriented websites are just technically enhanced versions of old-fashioned pornography. Like visual pornography, it debases those who offer it and those who use it. All pornography—including the aural telephone variety—is designed to maximize gratification and minimize personal relationship. This is why pornographers often disguise their identities. For pornography to work, it has to create a distance between real persons. This is completely at odds with the meaning of Christian sex, which God gave us in order to create unity between two persons.

It is also important to note the highly addictive nature of some kinds of pornography. Occasional and experimental use of pornography by adolescents is the stuff of "B" movies and can be a normal part of growing up. For adults, however, even occasional use of pornography can be a symptom of marital problems. Repeated and habitual use of pornography—in print, over the phone, or on the screen—can signal serious psychological problems that need professional attention.

## What is the Church's position on sex aids?

There are aids to marital sex, such as certain kinds of clothing that serve to enhance us and make us look attractive and appealing. This is how Victoria's Secret makes its money—by making women look beautiful and sexy in a dignified and elegant way. There is nothing wrong with this. We all want to look our best. Even those who ordinarily don't care much about how they look or what they wear are going to make an effort to look their best on that special date. The same is true for spouses who want to give their very best selves in the act of marital lovemaking. God obviously intended the sexual act to involve pleasure, and there is no shame in "setting the stage" so the pleasure and enjoyment of this most intimate experience is all that it can be.

Other kinds of marital aids—things used during foreplay or intercourse—have risks. They can intrude upon or even replace the affection and mutuality that is essential to sexual love. Because the particular things that cause sexual arousal vary greatly from one person to another, an object or a device that is exciting to one person may be repulsive to his or her spouse. Certain objects or practices can cause pain, injury, or even disease, and their use can lead to violence or abuse. Clearly this is at odds with our understanding of marital sex as holy and sacramental.

It takes time for spouses to learn each other's sexual language. One partner may prefer certain caresses and touches, the other may prefer words or language. But sexual experience must always be centered on affirmation, sensitivity, and mutual love. If you do not find marital sex interesting unless it includes a blindfold, a whistle, and hot wax, you probably need to see a therapist and a priest, in that order.

The rule of thumb here is that the more a particular sexual activity excludes mutuality, the more suspect it is.

### Is it wrong to use Viagra or other things that enhance sexual performance?

Not necessarily. As television ads relentlessly instruct us, E.D. (erectile dysfunction or male impotency) is a real medical condition that may be the result of vascular problems, diabetes, or neurological disease. It is appropriate to treat this just as we would any other illness that impedes our normal enjoyment of life. As long as the medication does not have any risky side effects, it is perfectly licit.

There is a danger of becoming fixated on this problem so we lose all perspective and spend large sums of money, time, and energy trying to achieve the perfect sexual experience. One woman told me that she wished Viagra had never been invented. "All my husband does now is obsess about his performance," she said. "Doesn't he know I love him just the way he is?"

All men lose their sexual potency with age. While in some instances it may be advisable to address that diminishment with medications, it is important to remember there are many ways to express marital love. Above all, remember that married love is about persons, not performance.

## Is it wrong to have sexual fantasies? Sometimes I can't seem to control them.

Sexual fantasies, like many other things that float into consciousness, are often not willed nor even desired. Saint Augustine struggled with impure thoughts, and even St. Paul said he often failed to do what he wanted to do, and did exactly what he didn't want to do!

We often associate bad thoughts solely with sex, but we can have equally sinful thoughts about other things, too. Think, for example, of the intemperance that gives rise to road rage, or the prejudice that gives rise to racism, or the envy or jealousy that lead us to think uncharitable things about (or even do uncharitable things to) another person. Surely wishing harm for someone or fantasizing about how they might suffer misfortune is no worse than entertaining a bad sexual thought. In some kinds of fantasies we are tempted to hurt, repay, or offend someone. In our sexual fantasies, we are tempted to possess someone as an instrument of self-satisfaction.

From a moral point of view, however, it is not just *having* these thoughts—since they often arise involuntarily before we are even aware of them. The big problem is what we *do* with them once they occur. Do we dismiss them and think about something else, or do we invite them in and entertain them for a while? There is a big moral difference between the unbidden thoughts that sometimes possess us and willingly indulging them in order to arouse some passion, whether that passion is unchaste, unjust, or uncharitable.

I once asked a wise retreat director what to do about unwanted bad thoughts. He said his rule was, "Don't even go there." As soon as we're aware of these uncharitable or unchaste thoughts, we should change the topic and leave no room for them.

## A friend of mine belongs to a sexual-addiction group. How can a person be addicted to sex?

We have already noted that St. Thomas Aquinas and other early theologians were well aware of the power of the basic human desire for pleasure of taste (food and drink) and touch (sex). Desires for these pleasures seem to be more deeply rooted in us than desires for other things, and many of the capital sins (lust, gluttony, drunkenness) relate directly to these desires.

In recent years, we have learned a great deal about chemical addictions. We know that addiction to alcohol or drugs is not entirely free behavior; substance dependency is probably the result of genetic predisposition and can never be controlled. This is why Bill W., the founder of Alcoholics Anonymous, told his fellow alcoholics that the first step in recovery was to admit powerlessness. He said that while addictions were never cured, discipline and support from other people could result in a state of ongoing recovery. His twelve-step program enjoys great success and is very similar to the process that all of us go through as we acquire other virtues in our lives.

Psychiatrists realize that there is sexual behavior that exhibits characteristics very similar to substance abuse. For reasons that are not fully understood, some people become addicted to a compulsive sexual activity. Researcher John Money said this occurs when some inappropriate object or activity "trespasses" onto someone's "love map" during a critical period of sexual development and becomes imprinted there, like a footprint in wet concrete. The resulting desires are permanent and addictive. These addictive behaviors may include pornography, anonymous sex, marital infidelity, pedophilia, voyeurism, frotteurism (rubbing against strangers in public places), or exhibitionism. The consequences—guilt and remorse, missed work, ruined marriages, arrest, and disease—are every bit as destructive as alcoholism or drug addiction. A number of twelve-step programs have been developed to help persons who suffer from this kind of compulsive behavior to regain control of their lives and, like recovering substance abusers, live sober.

## Is rape about sex or anger?

Like any human action, rape can have many different motives. Sometimes it is about sex, especially so-called "date rapes." These often start out as ordinary encounters that become violent, sometimes because of misinterpreted signals, often because of drugs or alcohol. Men who commit these rapes simply lose control and allow their lust to take over.

In other cases, rape has little or nothing to do with sexual pleasure. Especially in serial crimes, rape is usually the result of warped sexual development that causes a man to find satisfaction in victimizing or humiliating women.

Sometimes therapists are able to trace this violence back to traumatic incidents involving women in early childhood, sometimes not. Anger rape can even occur in marriage, however, and it often goes unreported. Men with anger-management problems—especially if they are exacerbated by their own failures, by unemployment, or intoxication—often take out their own frustrations on the people they love. Unlike the criminal sociopath, this kind of sexual violence can sometimes be treated psychologically.

Sometimes rape is the result of deeply ingrained cultural attitudes. In December 2012, a shocking gang rape of a young woman in India that resulted in her death raised painful questions about attitudes toward women. A *Wall Street Journal* poll taken in January 2013 found that Indian men felt the prevalence of rape in India was the result of attitudes toward women, Western influence, and gaps in law enforcement, but there are many unanswered questions about the connection between social attitudes and rape.

# CHAPTER 3

# Questions About Marriage, Family, and Divorce

*The War of the Roses* (1989), a movie starring Kathleen Turner and Michael Douglas, portrays the dark and tragic dissolution of what started out as a prosperous and apparently happy marriage. Extreme even by Hollywood standards, this film shows two selfish and willful spouses intent on ending their marriage and destroying one another in the process. It is literally a fight to the death. As one reviewer said, "Once in a lifetime a movie comes along that makes you want to get married all over again. This is not it."

Not all divorces are as violent and conflicted as the one portrayed in this movie, but every divorce is painful and leaves lasting scars. When children are involved, the potential for harm is even greater. Yet social attitudes about divorce have changed dramatically in a very short period of time. Today at least 40 percent of all marriages end in divorce. While the incidence of divorce is somewhat lower among Catholics, it is still significant and much higher than it was in the past. Not all of this change is due simply to changing moral sensibilities. In some ways, people divorce more frequently today simply because they are able to do so. Through most of human history, marriage provided economic and social stability that was essential to life. People often lived in the same small community for their entire lives, so social and family bonds were much tighter. Women rarely worked outside the home, so only the wealthiest had resources that would enable them to leave their husbands. Furthermore, life expectancy was much shorter than it is today, so the purpose of marriage was far more focused on procreation than it is now. Today many marriages fail because partners fall out of love, get bored, or grow and develop in such a way that the person they married is no longer interesting to them. If there were no economic security outside of marriage, they would have to make it work.

Changes in the family are no less significant. "Family" once meant a husband, a wife, children, and perhaps one or more grandparents. Today families may consist of one parent, two unmarried parents, a grandparent, or two same-sex parents. In second or third marriages, "family" may involve children from previous marriages or children who are awkwardly divided between two parents who live apart. All but the most mature children can't help asking themselves if somehow it was their fault, and they may carry that doubt—and anger toward their divorced parents—long into adulthood.

There are clearly no perfect families. All families are human and are made up of fallible persons who are subject to many different kinds of external stresses. Ordinary economic and job-related stress can put pressure on family life. When these stresses are compounded by serious illness, the death of a child, or unemployment, the cracks in family life can suddenly become chasms.

Finally, the notion of marriage itself is being redefined. Longer lives, economic security, and mobility have enabled people to see marriage as a serial activity rather than a lifelong commitment. While most people enter marriage with the intention of permanence, the opportunities and social approval of divorce make it too easy to give up.

Since Massachusetts legalized gay marriage in 2004 and the Iowa Supreme Court ruled that it is unconstitutional to deny two people of the same sex the right to marriage in 2009, nine states plus the District of Columbia have legalized gay marriage, and ten other states recognize some kind of same-sex union. In 2013, the United States Supreme Court allowed California to resume same-sex marriage and also declared that federal benefits may not be denied to same-sex spouses.

These legal developments occurred despite vigorous opposition by various religious groups, including the Catholic Church.

Francis Cardinal George said in a statement in early 2013 that marriage is not just a religious question. "It comes to us from nature, and neither the Church nor state can change it," he said. He said gay marriage jeopardizes the natural relationship between parents and children and that its legalization, like the legalization of abortion, will move it from the category of immoral to a precondition of human freedom.[13]

Despite these cogent objections, it is likely that this trend toward the liberalization of attitudes toward gay marriage will continue. The ultimate effect of legal gay marriage remains to be seen, but it seems to signal a turning point in the way we understand marriage in general. The Church cannot unilaterally change civil law, but we can improve religious education (for children and adults) so that we foster a deeper understanding of what marriage should be. Perhaps the best hope is that heterosexual couples will see greater value in their own marriage commitments if they know that others are fighting with such determination for the same privilege.

### Why can't we have sex before we're married? We're in love and engaged. Is this just to keep us under Church control?

We've already spoken about sex as a language or a self-speaking. Like other kinds of speech, sexual language should be honest and marked by integrity. It is a privileged kind of speaking, and its words are only spoken in privileged places. An actor does not stand in the middle of a bus station and scream his lines for all to hear. He speaks them only in the carefully arranged setting of the theater. Similarly, the verdict of a judge is not whispered in a dark corner but spoken clearly in a formal setting known as a courtroom. Huge business deals are not made in a football stadium during the fourth quarter but in a business meeting marked by respect and trust.

Similarly, when we engage in sex, it must only be at certain times and in certain protected places so that intimacy and trust will allow such "words" to be spoken.

It is possible, of course, that the intimacy, trust, and commitment necessary to support these words are present before marriage. But marriage is a social event and should be publicly recognized. The Church's insistence that sex should occur only in marriage is based on our belief that sex is not just a private, personal reality. It is also a public reality that has consequences for others besides the two people who are in love. When I celebrate marriages, I often talk about how the married couple is becoming a "home for others." They are getting married because they love one another and want to share their lives together, but the people in the pews—the witnesses—also have a stake in this marriage. It is a public vow. Even their sexual lives as a married couple will have a public meaning as they bear and raise their children.

### We are about to start marriage preparation. If we tell the priest we are living together, will he refuse to marry us?

Not necessarily. Couples who begin marriage preparation come from very diverse backgrounds. Some have been married and divorced; some have been married and lost a spouse to death. Others are old and have never married; still others are young and are experiencing true love and the desire for marriage for the first time. So priests and others who do marriage preparation are accustomed to hearing a lot of different life histories. A history of living together is only one of them.

Since this is such an important commitment, preparation should be marked by honesty. If you are or have been living together, that should be included in a candid conversation between you and the pastor or other minister who is doing marriage preparation with you. You will likely be asked to talk about what led you to the choice to live together in the first place: Was it convenience, lack of options, finances? Did you actually decide at all? Sometimes couples just find themselves living together. When asked to reflect upon it, they realize that they never made a clear decision to do so. You may be asked to talk about what "together" meant to you, and how it is different from marriage. You may be asked to live apart for some time as a way of demonstrating that you understand that life changes once you actually get married.

## If, for economic reasons, a couple wants to purchase a home together before they are married, is it permissible for them to live together?

In the not-too-distant past, it would have been rare to find an unmarried man and a woman living together as roommates. Today, however, it is fairly common. Sometimes these living arrangements are dictated by finances—a homeowner or renter finds he or she just can't afford to live alone so looks for a compatible roommate. Other times it is a result of friendship. In many ways this is a positive development—it shows that we have learned to have intimate friendships that do not involve sex.

So in principle, a couple could buy a home together before marriage as an economic strategy. There's nothing immoral about inhabiting the same home. However, when a joint real-estate venture is more than just a business deal and involves eventual marriage, there are hazards. Above all, it is important for the couple to be very clear about what they are doing. Buying a home is a huge commitment. They need to remember that real estate is one commitment, marriage is another, and they are not interchangeable. It would be easy for one partner to insist on the house for economic reasons when in fact joint purchase is really an attempt to seal the marriage deal in advance.

Buying a house together could create pressure for marriage and make it difficult to back out if you have a change of heart. Such arrangements are full of possibilities for misunderstanding, disappointment, and anger. Unless it is very clear that joint home ownership is—until marriage—just a business deal (and clear legal contracts are drawn up to protect both parties), it is not advisable.

**My husband wants to have sex every other day.**
**We have three young children, and I'm just too tired.**
**Is it wrong for me to refuse?**

You're not the first to ask this question. When St. Paul was preaching to the Corinthians, someone apparently asked the same thing. Paul says, "The husband should give to his wife her conjugal rights and likewise the wife to her husband....Do not deprive one another except perhaps by agreement for a set time, to devote time to prayer...so that Satan may not tempt you..." (1 Corinthians 7:3 and 5, *New Revised Standard Version*).

Saint Paul's advice came to be known as "rendering the marital debt," and we find similar advice in Jewish sources. This advice was based on two things. First of all, sexual relations are the living symbol of two becoming one flesh. Marriage is not just a spiritual reality but a physical one. Couples demonstrate that; they make their marriage sacramental by allowing their physical intimacy to be an occasion of grace.

But as St. Paul obviously knew, we all have urges and desires, and if we can't satisfy them at home, we might start looking elsewhere. So he gives very practical advice, telling the married couples in his congregation in Corinth not to deprive one another, except "for a set time."

Unfortunately, not everyone's libido is on the same clock. So out of charity and mutual concern, married couples should try to accommodate one another even when they don't feel like it. It is just another way in which couples support each other and go the extra mile required by love. There are certainly cases, however, when fatigue, illness, or other factors make it impossible to enter into sexual intimacy honestly. In those cases, a spouse should be candid. If disparate sexual needs are a chronic problem, the couple should see a marriage therapist. Sometimes this kind of sexual incompatibility is a symptom of more serious marital problems.

## What does it mean to say that marriage is a sacrament?

A sacrament is a symbol. It is a touch, a pledge, or an action that in a mysterious and not fully comprehensible way effects what it signifies. This means that each sacrament uses some real, tangible thing to both signify and cause a certain effect. For example, the sacrament of baptism uses water, which everyone understands to be cleansing and refreshing. In baptism, water signifies the fact that in baptism we are cleansed of sin and made new because we are brought into the body of Christ.

Similarly, in the Eucharist, we use bread and wine, which are basic sources of human nourishment. So in the Eucharist, bread and wine signify nourishment, but they also cause us to be nourished and sustained in grace.

The sacrament of matrimony differs from other sacraments in a number of ways. First, the matter or the sign of the sacrament is the married couple and the words of commitment they speak to one another. As they approach each other and speak their vows, their actions signify a much deeper commitment they make to each other for the rest of their lives. Just as in baptism the water becomes a source of forgiveness and eternal life, so in matrimony the words of commitment signify a human promise that is made full and holy by the grace of God.

Another important difference is the duration of the sacrament of matrimony. Some sacraments, like reconciliation or the anointing of the sick, are relatively short in duration. Reconciliation, for example, involves confession, absolution, and penance; the anointing of the sick involves prayers, laying on of hands, and anointing. Matrimony, however, only begins with the vows couples make to one another. The sacrament extends throughout their lives as they grow in love and fidelity to one another. Their human love and commitment become an occasion for God's grace through the entire length of their marriage. Furthermore, this grace permeates all aspects of their marriage, even the explicitly sexual ones. Theologian Philip S. Keane notes:

Everything about marriage, including its explicitly sexual aspects, is part of the sacrament. Sometimes there is too much of a tendency to think of the sacrament of matrimony as the ceremony that begins the marriage; past fear of human sexuality may have been part of the reason why the marriage ceremony, rather than the whole marriage, popped into mind when we spoke about "sacrament." But all the married couple's giving to one another and to their children are part of the sacrament...Sexual intercourse, as a major sign of the union of the spouses, is surely to be conceived of as a major element in the sacramental life of the couple...in this context, it can be understood as a liturgical or worshipful action.[14]

The role of the priest also differs in the sacrament of matrimony. In other sacraments, a priest or deacon officiates or celebrates the sacrament. In matrimony, the priest does not bestow the sacrament on the recipient(s) as he does in Eucharist or reconciliation. The man and woman are the celebrants; it is they who bestow it upon one another. Through their love and affection, they cause grace in one another's lives just as the priest, acting in the person of Christ, "causes" the grace of reconciliation or baptism. The priest or deacon is an official witness, but in the end this sacrament is something the two spouses, with God's grace, do for one another.

## What is the difference between annulment and divorce?

Divorce is the legal dissolution of a marriage that once existed. In the past, marriages often had to go to court where a judge determined whose fault it was; we actually used to say that someone sued for divorce—petitioned the court to dissolve the marriage because of infidelity or some other serious problem. Since then, most states have developed no-fault divorce laws so that a couple can amicably and peacefully end their marriage.

We noted above that marriage is a sacrament that uses the human reality of love and commitment as an occasion of grace. The fuller and more real this human good is, the more fully it makes grace manifest. Because the essence of marriage is commitment, the *Catechism* states that "the Lord Jesus insisted on the original intention of the Creator who willed the marriage be indissoluble" (*CCC* 2382). The Church views marital vows as sacred and unbreakable as long as they were made freely and with the full consent of both parties. If for some reason that freedom is later determined to have been lacking, or if it can be demonstrated that one partner or the other did not actually consent to marriage as a lifelong commitment, the marriage can be annulled, or determined never to have existed. This is different from the dissolution of marriage that takes place in civil divorce.

Although the *Catechism* describes divorce as a grave offense "because it introduces disorder into the family and into society" (*CCC* 2385), it does allow that "if civil divorce remains the only possible way of ensuring certain legal rights, the care of the children, or the protection of inheritance, it can be tolerated" and is not sinful (*CCC* 2383).

Either partner in a failed marriage may petition the Church for an annulment if he or she believes that there were impediments, coercion, lack of maturity, or misunderstanding that may have invalidated the consent given in the wedding vows. To avoid legal complications, the Church will not consider an annulment petition until the couple has obtained a civil divorce.

### Does the Church allow divorce if the spouse is abusive?

The Church does not require that someone remain in an abusive marriage. Marriage is a sacrament that must be built upon trust and respect. That obviously cannot occur when either party is abusive. Women are usually (but not always) the victims of marital abuse. Often the first step is the most difficult. It can be hard for a victim even to acknowledge abuse, much less take steps to escape it. Family pressure, shame, or concern for children often lead victims to tolerate abuse far longer than they should.

Fortunately, many agencies and private organizations can help the abuse victim recognize the reality of abuse and, if necessary, find shelter for her and her children. Such shelter and other services help the abuse victim start a new life. These services are available on a short-term, emergency basis or for longer periods of times.

In an abusive relationship, counseling is the first option; if this is not successful, separation is the next step, but this is often hard to achieve without help. Divorce is a last resort that may be the only option in some cases. In cases of abuse, especially if abuse began early in the marriage or even before marriage, the abused spouse may have adequate grounds to petition for annulment once the divorce is final.

### Can someone who is sterile or who has had a hysterectomy get married in the Church?

Yes. While the Church requires a married couple to be open to procreation and to take no active steps to frustrate fertility, pre-existing sterility in either the husband or wife is not an impediment to marriage. If a couple is considering marriage in the face of sterility, however, they should discuss carefully what this will mean to their marriage. While there are clearly other avenues of generativeness for the couple, adoption being one, procreation is a primary end of marriage. The permanent absence of procreation can place great strain on a marriage. Couples who will not be able to procreate naturally should carefully consider whether they are mature enough to accept this and whether they are creative enough to find other ways in which their marital love may bear fruit.

### If I had premarital sex and contracted a disease, should I inform someone before I start dating?

If you have a sexually transmitted disease, the first thing you should do is see a doctor and get treatment. After that, there's no need to disclose your entire medical history on the first date. You should never engage in sexual activity if you think you carry a sexually transmitted disease.

Dating couples should get to know each other gradually, and you don't want to disclose personal facts of life in a way that is inappropriate to your level of intimacy. If your relationship becomes more prolonged and serious, you should disclose any serious illness or propensity to illness. Your date has a right to this information, and you have a right to know that progress in your relationship is not based on false pretenses. This also applies to any medical problems that may affect fertility. There is an appropriate time to share this information before the relationship becomes too serious.

Before marriage or after, it is a serious violation of charity and justice to expose your partner to sexually transmitted disease.

## Why can't people who have been divorced receive Communion?

The fundamental moral issue here is scandal, or the possibility that others will misunderstand or misinterpret our actions in a way that their own faith will be weakened. In the cases of divorce and annulment, there are a number of ways in which this can happen.

The first would be the case of a person who was divorced, petitioned for and received an annulment, and then remarried. Once the annulment has been granted, that person is free to remarry and receive the sacraments. In some cases, however, fellow parishioners may know only about the divorce and not be privy to the fact that an annulment was obtained. "Since when is it OK to divorce, remarry, and still receive Communion?" they might ask, unaware of the annulment. Even though this is in no way the fault of the couple, who have done everything correctly, it can still create a pastoral problem.

A second case involves a person who was divorced but did not even seek an annulment. If the reason for not seeking an annulment was disregard for Church teaching or for the permanence of marriage, this is cause for scandal, especially if the person continues to receive Communion. Since the Church does not recognize civil divorce, the person who remarries without an annulment is effectively "living in sin." If the circumstances become widely known in the parish, it may be appropriate for the pastor to address the situation.

A final case is the person who divorces, petitions for but fails to receive an annulment, but remarries anyway. In such a case it may be that the vows of the first marriage were valid and freely given. In this case, the person actually is not free to remarry.

Or it may be that there was indeed an invalidating impediment that actually rendered the marriage null, but this could not be proven through external evidence offered to the marriage tribunal. Lacking evidence, the tribunal might deny the request for annulment, even though, in fact—if the truth could be clearly seen—the marriage was never validly consented to.

In this case, a person of goodwill, with a well-formed conscience, may consult with a pastor or spiritual director and make the determination that before God he was never married and choose to remarry and continue to receive the sacrament. This is known as the "internal forum" solution. It is a risky step because it takes a person outside of the Church's law and external evidence; it can also cause scandal to others.

Because of the complexity of marriage and personal nature of sin and moral goodness, we should always be very cautious and charitable about judging the motives of the moral state of another's soul.

# CHAPTER 4

# Questions About Homosexuality and Sex Outside of Marriage

Everything we know suggests that homosexuality—and other variant sexual practices—have existed for a very long time. Yet the extent to which we acknowledge them or speak about them varies widely from one culture and time to another. For much of the last century or two, homosexuality was largely known as "the love that dare not speak its name" or as the "unspeakable vice." If spoken about at all, it was only spoken of in hushed tones. The stigma attached to homosexuality was so powerful that gay and lesbians were subject to discrimination and abuse. Sometimes in desperate isolation or shame, they took their own lives rather than face the consequences of being identified publicly.

In our own generation we have seen a dramatic change in the way we view homosexuality. Even the Church, which was often held responsible for negative cultural attitudes toward gay men and women, has made it clear in various documents that there is a distinction between the homosexual person, who is to be respected and loved, and homosexual acts, which are considered to be sinful. The *Catechism* states unequivocally that homosexual persons "must be accepted with respect, compassion, and sensitivity. Every sign of unjust discrimination in their regard should be avoided" (*CCC* 2358).

It should be clear from what we said about sexuality in general that it is a very complex reality. In one sense all of us are heterosexual, and all of us are also homosexual. We have the ability to know and love both male and female persons. The growing acceptance of homosexual persons has led many people—and even the Church—to worry that it will lead to an uncritical acceptance of sexual activity outside of marriage and perhaps even lead young people to choose what they perceive as a desirable lifestyle.

The *Catechism* also notes that while the number of homosexual persons is "not negligible," the origins of homosexuality are not clearly understood. This is true, although most experts agree that sexual identity or orientation (including homosexuality) is (a) the result of both biological and social factors; (b) is formed at an early age, perhaps before the onset of puberty; and (c) is usually permanent and very resistant to change.

Those who have done the most extensive research, especially John Money, MD, say that the development of sexual identity is not an "either/or" proposition—either nature on the one hand or environment (nurture) on the other. Rather, he says, it is the result of three things: certain biological influences that constitute nature; one or more critical periods in embryonic development or early childhood in which sexual identity is particularly subject to influence; and various experiences in early childhood that either reinforce or repudiate early influences. Before birth, the sexual development of our brains is influenced by hormones; after birth, by sensory experiences.[15] Although Money's theory leaves some unanswered questions, I am not aware of any other theory about the development of sexual identity that is more comprehensive. As I answer questions in the following section, I will assume that Money's hypothesis is true as far as it goes.

It is important to note that there are not one but several moral issues surrounding homosexuality. One is the moral status of homosexual persons; the second is the morality of homosexual acts, which take place in a variety of different situations; the third issue is that of civil and human rights for gay and lesbian persons. In some ways, this question is the most difficult and controversial matter we will deal with in this book.

### What is the relationship between homosexuality and pedophilia?

There is no inherent relationship between homosexuality and pedophilia. Despite the enormous publicity surrounding the sexual abuse of boys by priests, the incidence of pedophilia (sexual attraction to young children) appears to be distributed about equally among homosexuals and heterosexuals. In fact, most hard-core pedophiles often do not discriminate between boys and girls. Their sexual attraction is to children, whatever their gender may be.[16]

Because the sexual abuse of minors is often not reported, it is difficult to know how often it occurs. However, studies indicate that the sexual abuse of girls is more frequent than abuse of boys—sometimes two or three times higher. This suggests that while homosexual abuse of children certainly exists, the abuse of girls, especially within families, is a much more serious problem.

## Are homosexuality and bisexuality normal?

The answer to this question depends on how we define "normal." If we mean statistical normalcy, these two conditions constitute a small but fairly stable minority of the population, probably around 5 percent. The occurrence of homosexuality seems to be constant across cultures and even across history. The causes are not well understood, but like other kinds of sexuality it appears to be established well before puberty, possibly even before birth.

Polls indicate that homosexuality has steadily gained acceptance in society.[17] Openly gay persons have been elected to a variety of public offices, including Congress. There is no evidence that gay persons as a group are any less productive, intelligent, or capable of holiness than others. Most Americans now feel that one's sexual orientation does not necessarily have a negative effect on job performance or character. And as mentioned here, these attitudes reflect the Church's catechismal teaching that gay persons should be accepted unequivocally, with no hint of discrimination.

Still, the low incidence of homosexuality is a sign of the difficulties it presents. Awareness of homosexual attraction can be a painful discovery for children and adults; homosexual acts are in no way approved by the Church because they lack the complementarity and procreative potential that must mark all sexual relations.

So statistically, homosexuality is normal in the sense that it seems to occur regularly among diverse populations, but it is abnormal because it affects only a small number of persons. It is normal in the sense that it does not necessarily impede maturity, holiness or productivity; but it is abnormal because it lacks the possibility of procreation and the male-female complementary that are the basis of sexual morality.

## Does the Church consider homosexuality a sin?

Although Church teaching considers the homosexual orientation to be disordered because homosexual acts are closed to the gift of life and lack the "affective and sexual complementarity" necessary for marriage, the Church nonetheless clearly affirms the basic human dignity of homosexual persons and their ability to achieve graced and holy lives.

We have already noted scientific evidence that suggests that in the vast majority of cases sexual identity—homosexual, heterosexual or somewhere in between—is not a matter of choice. It is determined before we are even aware of it, and we gradually grow into it as we mature. So even if there is an essential imperfection in homosexuality because of the lack of complementarity and inability to procreate, gay persons are in no way morally responsible for their orientation. They should not see it as an obstacle to a fulfilling and happy life.

It follows from this that a homosexual inclination is in no way incompatible with a Christian vocation or the pursuit of holiness. All of us have various inclinations to sin, and gay persons have the same hope of God's friendship and grace as anybody else.

## What does the Church mean by "intrinsically evil" acts?

The *Catechism* describes rape as "an intrinsically evil act" and says that homosexual acts are "intrinsically disordered." The word "intrinsic" means "inherent"—meaning that these acts, by their very nature, regardless of circumstances or intention, are always wrong. This is important because there are some actions that, although morally neutral in themselves, can become seriously immoral depending on the circumstances. For instance, if someone asks if sexual intercourse is immoral, the answer would be, "It depends." The act of intercourse is morally neutral in itself; it is neither good nor bad until we know the answers to several questions: who, where, when, and why.

These acts are not just wrong because someone says so but because they are fundamentally at odds with what it means to be human. Intrinsically evil acts, on the other hand, are always objectively morally wrong, regardless of the circumstances. Rape is wrong because it is a violation of human dignity and freedom. Homosexual acts are judged to be disordered because they lack the proper finality or goal of procreation and union between a man and a woman.

## What should I do if I learn one of my children is homosexual?

Because sexual identities, or at least tendencies, are established early in life, parents sometimes suspect that a child may be gay. Choice of games or companions or clothing sometimes give hints, but parents should not jump to conclusions. Children go through various stages of affection and learn gradually what love and sexual attraction mean. Statements or behavior that might seem to indicate homosexuality may be just a child's clumsy attempt to sort out love from attraction or to figure out how boys or girls "are supposed to act." Parents should be circumspect about them and not react with alarm.

Whatever orientation a child ultimately ends up with, the love and support of parents is critical. Parental overreaction is unwarranted and often destructive. It can make a child fearful of honesty and cause him or her to begin to compartmentalize life and perhaps even to lie to parents. This can eliminate candid dialogue and make it impossible for parents to have any further role or influence in the child's life.

In 1997, the U.S. Conference of Catholic Bishops issued a pastoral letter titled *Always Our Children*. Directed at the parents of gay and lesbian children, this document acknowledges that parents may become aware of their child's homosexuality in a number of ways; it also notes that typically parents experience varied and conflicting emotions: relief that is it finally out in the open, protectiveness, anger, mourning, fear, shame, or embarrassment.

The bishops offer advice that I could hardly improve upon. They say that parents should:

1. Accept and love yourselves as parents in order to accept and love your son or daughter. Do not blame yourselves for a homosexual orientation in your child.

2. Do everything possible to continue demonstrating love for your child. However, accepting his or her homosexual orientation does not have to include approving of all related attitudes and behavioral choices. In fact, you may need to challenge certain aspects of a lifestyle that you find objectionable.

3. Urge your son or daughter to stay joined to the Catholic faith community. If the child has left the Church, urge him or her to return and be reconciled to the community, especially through the sacrament of penance.

4. Recommend that your son or daughter find a spiritual director/mentor to offer guidance in prayer and in leading a chaste and virtuous life.

5. Seek help for yourself, perhaps in the form of counseling or spiritual direction, as you strive for understanding, acceptance, and inner peace. Also, consider joining a parents' support group or participating in a retreat designed for Catholic parents of homosexual children.

6. Reach out in love and service to other parents struggling

with a son or daughter's homosexuality. Contact your parish about organizing a parents' support group.

7. As you take advantage of opportunities for education and support, remember that you can only change yourself. You can only be responsible for your own beliefs and actions, not those of your adult children.

8. Put your faith completely in God, who is more powerful, more compassionate, and more forgiving than we are or ever could be.

Pope Francis reiterated this advice when he was asked if he approved of homosexuality. He said he replied with another question: "Tell me: When God looks at a gay person, does he endorse the existence of this person with love, or reject and condemn this person? We must always consider the person. Here we enter into the mystery of the human being. In life, God accompanies persons, and we must accompany them, starting from their situation." This means that whether it is gay children or gay friends, we accompany them on their journey of salvation, helping them to find God's grace in the details of their lives.

## If I think I am gay, should I marry someone of the opposite sex to get rid of those feelings?

No. There are two problems with this. First of all, marrying a person in order to settle a question about who you are is using a prospective spouse as a therapeutic tool and a means to an end. It would be saying, "I'll marry this person in order to resolve my own anxiety." Doing so would also involve deception—at least about your own doubts. That is clearly not a good basis on which to build a lifelong commitment of love.

The second problem is that if in fact you turn out to be gay, you have done your spouse a serious injustice. In fact, it might even invalidate your marriage vows, since you would not have been fully free to pledge lifelong love and sexual affection to the person you married. Your marriage vows would be on very shaky ground because you would be making them without the physical attraction that is part of married sexual life. Bringing children into a marriage that is destabilized by doubts about your sexual identity would constitute a further injustice.

If attraction to persons of the same sex or experiences of homosexual activity make you question your sexual identity, do not move further into a heterosexual romance. Put that on hold and see a therapist who can help you sort out your conflicting feelings.

## What if I am already married and have homosexual feelings?

This is a more complicated problem, because you have made a serious commitment to your spouse, and you may also have children. It is important not to make matters worse. If you are having homosexual feelings, or even if you are convinced that in fact you are homosexual, you should not engage in any sexual activity outside your marriage. This is not only dishonest but exposes your spouse to the possibility of contracting a sexually transmitted disease.

The first step should be to have a candid conversation with your spouse; be as honest as you can and seek his or her support. Then find a qualified therapist who can help you explore your feelings. Sometimes, especially for women, feelings of deep affection for another person of the same sex can be confused with sexual attraction.

It is sometimes possible for a gay man or woman to remain in a heterosexual marriage, but it requires a great deal of effort, honesty, and support from a spouse. This option, from a moral perspective, is the most desirable, but it may not be possible for many people. In that case, separation, annulment, and divorce may be advisable. Your pastor can help you examine the alternatives.

## A good friend recently told me he is gay and plans to marry his partner. Would it be wrong to continue to invite him to our home?

It is important to avoid reducing any person—straight or gay—to his or her sexual identity. Therefore, in a situation like this one, the first thing to remember is that this person is the same person you grew to love as a friend. Perhaps now more than ever, he needs your continued friendship and support. The fact that he is gay should not alter your respect for him. If you find his relationship objectionable, you should tell him that, but make it clear that he is still a valued friend.

None of us can survive without friendships; indeed they are the most important aspects of human life. The relationship your friend has with his partner is first and foremost a friendship, and it should be respected and valued like any other friendship. You may find the possibility of their sexual relationship disturbing, but you should not dwell on it as if that were the only pertinent fact. Just as you would not inquire of heterosexual friends who are dating and hoping to marry about whether they are having sex or not, similarly you should not speculate about whether or in what ways your friend and his partner relate to one another sexually.

You are not obliged, however, to accommodate sleeping arrangements that you find objectionable, and your friend should not presume upon your willingness to do so. Also, if you have children and your friend and his partner visit, you must be prepared for questions that arise. Unless your children are old enough to understand the complexities involved, his partner should be introduced as just a friend and no more.

## What does it mean to be bisexual? Is bisexuality morally acceptable?

We have already suggested that sexual identity is established very early in life, that it is permanent, and that it involves both brain development before birth and learned behavior after. Sexual identity is not just straight or gay. Human sexuality is complicated and falls along an entire spectrum from totally heterosexual to totally homosexual. There are a number of possibilities in between.

Bisexuality is the term used to describe persons who experience sexual attraction to persons of both genders. Persons who have bisexual inclinations are not physically bisexual; they are clearly male or female, but they do have a wider range of affection than most of us do.

There is nothing immoral about bisexual attraction in itself, but it is obviously not acceptable for someone who is bisexual to have sexual relationships with both men and women. Although it would be rare for someone to be equally attracted to men and women, it is theoretically possible. Persons who are truly bisexual must opt for heterosexuality in order to build a life of integrity and honesty.

## What is the Church's position on transgender persons and sex-change surgery?

In 1952, George William Jorgensen, who recently returned from a tour of duty in the Second World War, was concerned about the inadequate development of his male genitalia. He sought medical help and eventually made news by undergoing the world's first sexual reassignment process. George became Christine, and the rest is history.

Since then, advances in psychiatry, surgical techniques, and hormonal therapy have made such transformations much more common. Sometimes, as in Jorgensen's case, they are the result of inadequate or ambiguous formation of the genitals. When this is observed at birth, a determination has to be made about whether the newborn is really a boy or a girl. Sometimes it can take years to make this determination, and in some cases surgery is required to make the physical and mental sex of the child coincide.

In other cases there is no physical ambiguity, but the child growing up becomes insistent that he or she wants to be the opposite sex. The individual may adopt clothing, customs, or even names of the opposite sex. In adulthood, this may lead to the same process Jorgensen experienced. A number of medical centers in the United States have reassignment programs, and candidates are carefully screened before they are admitted.

Sexuality is both physical and mental. Most of us are both physically and mentally male or female. In some cases, however, prenatal influences may cause anomalies in genital formation so that there is a disparity between one's physical sex and one's "brain sex." The result is that even though I may physically look like one sex, my brain tells me I am another. Until recently, there was not much that could be done about this; the medical reality of gender dysphoria was not even recognized, let alone treatable.

Today we know that gender dysphoria (discontent with the biological sex you were born with) may be a symptom of the medical condition known as gender identity disorder. This condition is not immoral in itself, but persons who experience this must get full medical, psychological, and spiritual advice before embarking on the long, traumatic, and expensive process of gender reassignment.

# CHAPTER 5
# Questions About Reproduction, Family Planning, and Abortion

In 1347, Caterina Benincasa was born in Siena, Italy. She was the twenty-fourth of twenty-five children born to her parents, Giacomo and Lapa Benincasa. Eventually she would become famous as St. Catherine of Siena, the woman who boldly went to Avignon to urge the Pope to return to Rome, but the circumstances of her birth were not that unusual. High infant mortality and short life expectancy often required that women get pregnant as many times as possible. Unlike today, when children are an economic liability that must be carefully planned for, in St. Catherine's day (and for much of human history) children were an economic advantage. Without Social Security, IRAs, and assisted living, parents would never have been able to survive without the help of their adult children.

Things had changed a great deal by 1932, when Aldous Huxley wrote his famous book *Brave New World*. Although Huxley didn't know about genetics (the gene structure of the human person was not discovered until later), he did envision a world state in which reproduction was fully mechanized, in an assembly-line process called "Fordism." The novel opens in London...

...in the "year of our Ford 632" (2540 AD). In this world, the vast majority of the population is unified under The World State, an eternally peaceful, stable global society in which goods are plentiful and everyone is happy. In this society, natural reproduction has been done away with and children are decanted and raised in Hatcheries and Conditioning Centres. Society is divided into five castes, created in these centres. The highest caste is allowed to develop naturally while it matures in its "decanting bottle." The lower castes are treated to chemical interference to arrest intelligence or physical growth. The castes are Alphas, Betas, Gammas, Deltas, and Epsilons, with each caste further split into Plus and Minus members.

Recreational heterosexual sex is an integral part of society. In The World State, sex is a social activity rather than a means of reproduction and is encouraged from early childhood; the few women who can reproduce are conditioned to take birth control. The maxim "everybody belongs to everyone else" is repeated often, and the idea of a traditional family is repellent. As a result, sexual competition and emotional, romantic relationships are obsolete. Marriage, natural birth, the notion of being a parent, and pregnancy are considered too obscene to be mentioned in casual conversation.[18]

When it was written, Huxley's book was considered science fiction. No one really imagined that the technology for such a world would exist in the foreseeable future. By 1960, however, that world began to materialize with the availability of the pill—readily available oral contraception. Although this was not quite what Huxley envisioned, it did begin a process of separating procreation from sexual love.

1978 was another milestone year. In that year, Louise Brown was born in England, the first (or at least the first known) "test-tube baby" who was brought into existence in the laboratory completely apart from her parents' sexual relationship.

In 1996, yet another scientific milestone was achieved when Dolly, the first cloned sheep, was born. Although human cloning is not yet possible, science is advancing every day, and the first human clone is an inevitable certainty. How will the Church deal with this? Is our moral tradition, the eternal verities, the "old-time religion" many of us grew up with able to meet the challenges of this galloping technology?

Through all of this change, the Church has held fast to several principles that are deeply rooted in the way in which we understand the human person. We have already described the first principle, namely, the centrality of integrity and wholeness to Catholic morality. Every moral decision we make should reflect the wholeness that God implanted in us at creation. Solid moral choices will always acknowledge this wholeness and aim at greater wholeness and integrity.

Morality as wholeness also requires that sex should only occur in marriage, both to protect the couple from pain as they separate their physical and emotional selves, and also to protect any children who might result.

Finally, wholeness requires that even within marriage, the two aspects of sexual love—marriage and procreation—should never be deliberately separated. To do so violates the essential wholeness of the person willed by God. As Pope Paul VI wrote in his 1968 encyclical *Humanae Vitae*:

> This particular doctrine, often expounded by the magisterium of the Church, is based on the inseparable connection, established by God, which man on his own initiative may not break, between the unitive significance and the procreative significance which are both inherent to the marriage act. The reason is that the fundamental nature of the marriage act, while uniting husband and wife in the closest intimacy, also renders them capable of generating new life—and this as a result of laws written into the actual nature of man and of woman. And if each of these essential qualities, the unitive and the procreative, is preserved, the use of marriage fully retains its sense of true mutual love and its ordination to the supreme responsibility of parenthood.

This means that a couple may take advantage of naturally occurring periods of infertility, but they may not deliberately cause infertility, impede ovulation or fertilization, or prevent implantation of the fertilized embryo.

## Why is it wrong for a married couple to use contraception if they are just trying to time the birth of their children?

There are three ways to think about the Church's prohibition regarding the use of contraception, even in the context of marriage. The first way of thinking about it has to do with the nature of the marital act itself, that is, the God-given purpose of the act. As the Church understands it, God willed that the marital act have two integral and inseparable purposes: the unitive and the procreative. To separate these integral ends of the marital act is, according to Church teaching, to go against God's will.

Another way of thinking about this is rooted in how we understand sexuality and married love. In an earlier question, we noted that morality is really a question of wholeness and integration. Sin often involves choosing a lesser good than we are capable of, and that leads us to becoming less than we can truly be. The truly holy person is a whole person, someone whose physical, emotional, and spiritual self is unified. In marriage and in marital sex, spouses give their entire selves to one another without reservation, without holding anything back. When we deliberately frustrate the procreative aspect of marital sexuality, we are holding back, not giving of ourselves unreservedly. The contraceptive becomes a barrier between two persons, and the act is not marked by full self-giving. Pope Paul VI addressed this in *Humanae Vitae:*

> [L]ove...is total—that very special form of personal friendship in which husband and wife generously share everything, allowing no unreasonable exceptions and not thinking solely of their own convenience. Whoever really loves his partner loves not only for what he receives, but

loves that partner for the partner's own sake, content to be able to enrich the other with the gift of himself.

A third argument against artificial contraception is a common-sense one: If you don't need medical intervention, don't use it. Just as we mostly prefer natural, organic foods, natural fabrics, and natural pesticides, we also prefer the most natural and least-invasive medical therapies possible. None of us would opt for surgery if a pill were just as effective or for chemotherapy if vitamins and a week of vacation were just as effective. Similarly, many means of artificial contraception (including the pill and intrauterine devices) have significant risks of side effects. From a purely medical perspective, the first choice for family planning should always be natural.

Natural Family Planning (NFP) is a general term that covers several different methods, all of which rely on the natural cycle of fertility rather than devices or medications. NFP has gotten a bad reputation because early forms of "Catholic contraception" used a calendar to estimate infertile periods in a woman's monthly cycle. The so-called "rhythm method" was not dependable because many women's cycles vary month to month.

Other methods, notably the Billings Method, are far more reliable because they use physical symptoms of fertility that are predictable and easy to identify with proper training and cooperation from both spouses.

## What about *in vitro* fertilization between a husband and wife?

While the Church views having, raising, and educating children as one of the primary and most worthy goals or purposes of marriage, it also teaches that the means used to achieve that goal must also be morally appropriate. The Church considers IVF, or *in vitro* fertilization (Latin for fertilization "in glass," or in a laboratory setting), to be a morally inappropriate means for attaining that goal for two reasons.

First, in practice, IVF almost always entails the creation of more embryos than can be implanted into a woman's uterus at one time. The reason that extra embryos are almost always created is in case some of them turn out to be of insufficient quality to use and in case the procedure as a whole is unsuccessful. In the event that some embryos are deemed unusable, they are simply destroyed. Moreover, with the creation of "spare embryos," the woman would not have to go through the process of producing and obtaining multiple eggs in a single cycle a second time in order to do a second round of IVF, should the process fail or should she decide to have more children. In the event that the process is successful, the extra embryos are cryopreserved, that is, frozen so as to be kept in a state of suspended animation in a storage facility and then later either allowed to thaw and are discarded or used for research. Either way, the process of IVF almost always results in the destruction of living human embryos that do not get implanted in the woman, which is considered morally equivalent to an abortion within Church teaching.

Second, just as the Church teaches contraception is wrong because it entails the willful separation of the natural ends of the marital act, the Church also teaches that IVF is wrong because it replaces the marital act itself as the means of getting pregnant. In other words, IVF supersedes or is used as a substitute for the act that God willed to be the genesis of new life. In a somewhat different way, then, IVF is wrong for much the same reason that contraception is, namely, that it separates the procreative and unitive ends of the marital act. Procedures that totally separate the act of procreation from the couple's marital love are seen as inherently inappropriate ways to bring a child into the world.

There are some forms of assisted reproductive technology that merely assist but do not replace or substitute for the marital act itself. While such procedures may not be inherently wrong according to Church teaching, cost is a factor that should be taken into account. Assisted reproductive technologies are expensive and usually require several attempts. Couples must consider whether this is a good use of their resources, especially if they already have children. From a spiritual perspective, couples must also be careful not to become obsessed with pregnancy so that they lose perspective and fail to see other expressions of marital generativity, such as adoption, that expand their marriage and provide a home to children who would not otherwise have one.

## Why does the Church oppose stem-cell research, especially when it has the potential to cure illnesses like Parkinson's disease?

Stem cells are unspecialized cells that have the ability to divide and produce a variety of more specialized cells. Although their potential is not fully understood, scientists hope that one day they can be coaxed into specific kinds of cells that can cure disease or repair diseased organs or tissue. Because some kinds of stem cells are found in our own bodies, using them against disease would not involve the problems of rejection that accompanies organ transplants.

In its 2008 statement *On Embryonic Stem Cell Research,* the U.S. bishops note notes that there are two kinds of stem cells. Adult stem cells come from umbilical cord blood, adult tissue, and placenta. The bishops say they "can be obtained without harm to the donor and without any ethical problem."

Embryonic stem cells, on the other hand, are obtained by destroying embryonic human beings in the first days of development. Since harvesting these cells involves the deliberate killing of human beings, obtaining or using this second kind of cell is immoral. Using tax money to finance research on this kind of cell makes all of us complicit in an evil act. This is why the Church has opposed extending federally funded stem-cell research beyond the stem cell lines that currently exist.

Further research on embryonic stem cells has great appeal because of the vast therapeutic potential that these cells appear to have. However, it is important to note that it is never permissible to sacrifice a human being for the good of others, no matter how great the potential good might be. The bishops clarify the hazards of this pragmatic approach when they say, "The same ethic that justifies taking some lives to help the patient with Parkinson's or Alzheimer's disease today can be used to sacrifice that very patient tomorrow, if his or her survival is viewed as disadvantageous to other human beings considered more deserving or productive."

Catholics should therefore promote further research on adult stem cells, which show great promise, and resist efforts to expand research that uses embryonic cells.

### Why is the Church against abortion? Shouldn't a woman be allowed to decide what to do with her own body?

It is true that each of us is the primary steward of our own body. Gratitude to God for our very existence causes us to maintain good health and to revere the gift we have been given. Saint Paul asks, "Do you not know that your body is a temple of the holy Spirit...?" (1 Corinthians 6:19). Out of gratitude to God who created us, we revere those temples by maintaining our health and living well.

In this sense, all of us must decide what to do with our own bodies. This is why, in health matters, competent adults make their own treatment decisions. We only delegate this authority to someone else if we are unable to exercise it for ourselves.

Abortion is a different kind of situation, however. It is one instance in which the decision is not just about a woman's own body. From the moment of conception, a new human life, separate from the mother's, comes into existence. Once that life exists, he or she has rights and is not just a part of the mother's body to be disposed of at will. This is one reason why sexual intercourse outside of marriage is so risky. When it results in pregnancy, a serious new responsibility is presented to the mother and the father.

Unfortunately, men who share responsibility for pregnancy

do not always accept their share of the burden, and the mother is often left to fend for herself and her child. Sometimes women feel that for economic, social, or emotional reasons they have no other choice but abortion. The deep polarization that exists between pro-life and pro-choice activists only makes matters worse, because it precludes the possibility of a rational discussion about what we *agree on* (for example, no one thinks abortion is a *good* thing).

Feminist Naomi Wolf wrote one of the best essays I have ever read on this topic. In it, she argues for a radical shift in the pro-choice movement's rhetoric:

> We need to contextualize the fight to defend abortion rights with a moral framework that admits that the death of a fetus is a real death; that there are degrees of culpability, judgment and responsibility involved in the decision to abort a pregnancy; that the best understanding of feminism involves holding women as well as men to the responsibilities that are inseparable from their rights; and that we need to be strong enough to acknowledge that this country's high rate of abortion can only be understood... as a failure.[19]

Wolf also recognizes that, in terms of public policy, the main problem is that there is no consensus about the moral status of the early embryo. If the early embryo is not a human person, then what is it? Is it nonhuman, prehuman, simply a biological mass, or what? Unable to enter into a moral dialogue that would give us a common ethic, we are reduced to arguing about whether abortion should be legal or not.

Catholic journalist Peter Steinfels recognizes this dilemma. He believes we have made real progress, but that in the future Catholics should have a three-part strategy: continue to argue for legal protection of the embryo from the earliest time for which there is broad public consensus; continue to argue persuasively in favor of a moral obligation to protect unborn life from conception; and strengthen our witness to the value of human life by our compassionate concern for the poor, the weak, the alien, and the outcast.[20]

However, whether abortion is legal or not, it is always morally wrong. Those who freely and knowingly choose abortion always commit a serious sin.

### My friend had an abortion when she was young. She wanted to have the baby, but others said she wasn't ready. She says she can never go to Communion again. Is she guilty of serious sin?

There are two aspects to this question. The first is whether, or to what extent, your friend is morally culpable for the abortion she had. Moral culpability, or guilt, for any sin exists only insofar as people knew what they were doing and did it freely and without coercion. If your friend had the abortion when she was very young, she may not have fully understood the implications of her pregnancy or actions. Her main concern should be the moral responsibility she may have for her own choices, starting with her choice to engage in the sexual activity that led to the pregnancy in the first place. That is something she can determine with the help of a priest or a spiritual director.

If she acted under coercion or manipulation—say, at her parents' or partner's insistence—her own moral guilt may be lessened. Indeed, anyone who encourages or pressures someone into having an abortion does so wrongly and bears moral responsibility for contributing to an immoral act. They, too, should seek God's forgiveness through the sacrament of reconciliation and make amends for any pain they caused.

The second issue is whether or not your friend should participate in the Eucharist. Even if she was old enough to act freely and understand what she was doing, she should not avoid church.

Many times the celebration of the Eucharist opens up avenues of grace that lead to clearer understanding, a change of heart, and the courage to seek reconciliation. Even serious sins can be forgiven so that she can be restored to full Communion with her church.

While she may not receive Communion if she is in a state of serious sin, you should by all means invite her to join you at Mass. Sometimes all we need is the encouragement and support of a friend in order to take the next step. Your invitation would be a great act of charity and friendship that might help relieve her of a great burden.

## How can abortion be legal if it is so clearly immoral?

Even though the Church's position on the morality of abortion is clear, there are other questions about its legality. It is important to note, first, that there is an important distinction between law and morality. Morality is an internal reality that is oriented to making us good and virtuous persons who are seeking personal perfection. I only become virtuous by my free choices of good things.

Civil law or public policy, on the other hand, is primarily oriented to public order and the common good. When legislators pass laws, they may hope that they contribute to the uprightness of citizens, but their first goal is to create circumstances in which people can live together in peace. While there are things that we consider to be both illegal and immoral (such as murder, theft, fraud), there are also things that are legal but immoral (gambling, abortion, drinking to excess) as well as things that are moral but illegal (like exceeding the speed limit). This shows that while there is clearly a relationship between legality and morality, they are not the same thing.

Both St. Augustine and St. Thomas Aquinas noted this distinction. Augustine used it when he argued that we should not try to abolish prostitution because it would be impossible. The most we should do, he said, was to try to limit it to certain times and places so as to keep it out of the mainstream of society. Aquinas used a similar argument when he asked whether we should tolerate the religious rites of unbelievers (which he clearly saw to be sinful). He recommended that we tolerate them legally, since to do otherwise might result in social unrest or riots, which would run counter to the very purpose of law, that is, to maintain public order.

Therefore, a Catholic may legitimately judge that for one reason or another it is unfeasible or impossible to eliminate abortion by making it illegal. One might judge, for example, that such a law is unenforceable, especially in the age of over-the-counter abortifacient drugs such as the "morning-after pill." Therefore it is theoretically possible for a Catholic, or any other person of goodwill who recognizes the moral evil of abortion, to tolerate its legality as long as that person also adopts another strategy that would reduce or eliminate this evil in society.

## Is it a sin to vote for a candidate who is pro-abortion?

If the candidate is truly pro-abortion, in the sense that he or she is promoting abortion for eugenic or population-control reasons (for example, if the candidate supports legislation that would mandate aborting every fetus that is found to have any kind of genetic defect), the answer is an emphatic yes. A vote for such a candidate would always involve the voter in the candidate's murderous intent. Such a vote could never be justified, no matter what the candidate's positions were on other issues.

Unfortunately, the situation is usually not so black-and-white. Candidates almost never describe themselves as pro-abortion. They prefer to say they are pro-choice, a slogan that can mean a number of different things. This kind of slogan is appealing to many candidates because it allows them to be purposely ambiguous about what they believe. This allows them to cast their nets widely and capture as many voters as possible.

So voters have to take particular care to discern a candidate's real position from among at least three distinct meanings of pro-choice. First, pro-choice may mean that the candidate sees no moral aspect to abortion at all. It is a private matter that is of no concern to others and certainly not subject to any legal restrictions. Voting for a candidate who holds this position would be morally unacceptable for anyone who believes abortion is a moral evil.

Second, pro-choice could mean that the candidate believes abortion is immoral on religious grounds but that this religious conviction should not be imposed on others who do not share his faith. Although this is a very popular position, I see it as a shaky, evasive, and disingenuous argument because the moral status of the embryo—which in reality is a person—is not just a religious question. Any reasonable person of goodwill can (and should) ask: Is the embryo a person or not? And if "it" is a person, then does "it" not deserve some kind of human rights? I would be hesitant to vote for a candidate who holds such a position.

A third possibility is a candidate who believes on religious or nonreligious grounds that the embryo is a person and that abortion is morally wrong. Yet this candidate may also believe that we cannot eliminate abortion by legislation and that a situation in which you have both abortion *and* a network of illegal and unsafe abortionists would be worse than the alternative. A voter might not share the candidate's assessment of the possibility of eliminating abortion by legal interdiction, but he could not fault him for this position as long as the candidate made it clear that abortion is a moral evil and proposed other means to reduce or eliminate it.

In July 2004, before his election as Pope, Joseph Cardinal Ratzinger issued a brief statement on the question of whether one might vote for a candidate who held such a position. Ratzinger said:

> A Catholic would be guilty of formal cooperation in evil and so unworthy to present himself for Communion were he to deliberately vote for a candidate *because of a candidate's permissive stand* on abortion or euthanasia; when a Catholic does not stand in favor or abortion or euthanasia,

but votes for the candidate for other reasons, it is considered remote material cooperation, which can be permitted in the presence of *proportionate reason* [italics my own].

The USCCB endorsed this approach in the document *Forming Consciences for Faithful Citizenship* in 2008, when the bishops said:

A Catholic voter cannot vote for a candidate who takes a position in favor of an intrinsic evil, such as abortion or racism, if the voter's intent is to support that position. In that case, the voter would be guilty of formal cooperation in a grave evil.

Therefore, a Catholic voter could, after conscientious deliberation, vote for such a candidate *as long as the vote is in spite of the candidate's permissive stance* on the legality of abortion. It goes without saying that a Catholic who does vote according to such a rationale would also have to be committed to some strategy other than legal interdiction to reduce or eliminate moral evils like abortion and euthanasia.

# Conclusion

## Sex and Spirituality

Many years ago, one of my theology professors said there was only one question in sexual ethics, namely, "What is the purpose of intercourse?" At the time I thought it couldn't be that simple, but I have learned over the years that this is really true. There are many reasons people have sex. Some are good, some are not so good, and others are despicable. Sexual ethics is really a process of separating one category from the other.

We know that one good reason for sex is procreation, which is a both a personal and social value. In fact, until recently the Church described procreation as the primary end of marriage and sexuality. Still, as theologian Francis W. Nichols has noted, there is a "surplus value" to sexuality, reasons why we engage in sex even if we have already raised a family (or were unable to have children for one reason or another).[21] Our sexuality serves procreation, but it also expresses tenderness and love; it nurtures friendships, builds communities and deepens our appreciation for beauty. Ronald Rolheiser elaborates on these many dimensions of sexuality:

> Sexuality is not simply about finding a lover or even finding a friend. It is about overcoming separateness by giving life and blessing it. Thus, in its maturity, sexuality is about giving oneself over to community, friendship, family, service, creativity, humor, delight and martyrdom so that with God, we can help bring life in the world.[22]

The danger of a small book like this one, especially if it is arranged in a question-and-answer format, is that it looks like a cookbook or an instruction manual. This would be a misunderstanding, because even though we have dealt with many specific questions about sex and sexuality, in the end, sexuality is a story and a personal narrative. Each of us could relate the story of our sexual selves. It would wind through our lives from puberty (or before if we could recall all the influences that made us who we are) through young adulthood, middle age, and finally to baldness and gray hair.

But this story is also a narrative of the action of grace in our lives. Our sexuality is intimately interwoven with our spirituality. Both are life stories; both are paths to God. Some of our sexual moments may have been awkward, embarrassing, or shameful; others may have been reverential, sacred, and holy. But all of them are part of who we are, and it is only through them that we can hope to come into the presence of God. So it is appropriate that we conclude this book with a discussion of spirituality, which holds all of these disparate sexual experiences together.

There are reasons why we don't readily associate the words "sex" and "spirituality." On the one hand, we often reduce sex to its physical aspects, as though it is no more than the proximity of two body parts that come together for a very utilitarian purpose. On the other, we tend to consider spirituality only from a narrowly spiritual aspect. We say "spirituality" as though it had nothing to do with the body, when in fact Christian spirituality is anchored to the fact of the Incarnation, in which God became incarnate in Jesus Christ. In doing so, Jesus did not just put on human nature like an overcoat; he *became flesh* and (except for sin) experienced everything we do—including, presumably, sexual attraction and temptation. This view of Jesus' humanity is unsettling to us; its portrayal in *The Last Temptation of Christ* and in *The Da Vinci Code* causes controversy and even scandal. How could Jesus have experienced those things?

Yet if Jesus became human in any sense we would recognize, how could he *not* have experienced these things? The fact of the Incarnation compels us to believe that our bodily selves, even though flawed by sin, are *good enough* to bear the weight of grace. Therefore, when we define spirituality, we must take care that it encompasses our bodies as well as our souls. One way of defining spirituality would be to say that it is a person's "way of standing in the world with reference to God." This means that we "stand" as real, physical persons in a real world, but we do so knowing that God is our source and our goal. Another way would be to say, in the words of Ronald Rolheiser, that spirituality is "what we do with the fire within us, the way we channel our *eros*." This definition has particular pertinence for this book, since *eros*, or sexual love, is one kind of powerful human desire. William E. May describes how the virtue of chastity does not destroy *eros*, but shapes it:

> Chastity does not seek to suppress or deny sexuality, but rather enables a person to put a loving and intelligent order into his passional life to take possession of his desires so that the whole self can be integrated and at peace.[23]

Still another possibility is to describe spirituality as the way in which grace is actualized in, or perfects, my personality. We have already noted that grace does not replace my personality and make me into some other unrecognizable person. Grace perfects who I am, making me fully the person God wants me to be. When grace perfects sexuality, it shapes it in such a way that it serves me and the people around me.

## Solitude and Sexuality

Sexuality involves creativity and union, but there are also moments when our love and desire will go unrequited or unsatisfied. All of us, even married couples, have moments of intense loneliness. Being lonely is not a good or pleasant experience, but we can learn to transform loneliness into solitude if we see it as a time to deepen our own self-love through prayer and self-reflection.

This may seem paradoxical, but we can only love others to the extent that we love ourselves because we are grateful to God for the gift of life. Writing about celibate spirituality, A.W. Richard Sipe observes:

> Prayer, self-knowledge and openness should lead quite naturally to an awareness of being loved—which flows into appropriate self-love. These are the two building blocks that undergird all celibate/sexual love. Again, it was Augustine who counseled, "First see whether you have learned to love yourself....If you have not learned how to love yourself, I am afraid you will cheat your neighbor as yourself." The Gospel message is consistent: "You are loved." We must apply this to ourselves before we can convince others of that good news.[24]

This cultivation of solitude and gratitude is something that vowed celibates, single persons, and married couples have in common. Solitude reminds us that we will never be completely fulfilled in this life. God created us ultimately for life together with God, and as St. Augustine says, "Our hearts are restless until they rest in God." When we experience loneliness and sexual desire, we need to remember that even though we were made for our eternal destinies, our bodies sometimes want to stop short of that and "rest" in something more proximate. The moments of loneliness we experience are opportunities to feel our need and our longing and to try to focus them on the God who called us into being, and who calls us back to union with him.

# Resources

The questions and answers in this book are brief and meant only to provide general guidelines. The following publications explore these questions at much more length and provide in-depth treatment of the issues raised in this book.

## Church Documents From the Holy See

The following are on the Vatican website, vatican.va:

*Humanae Vitae:* On the Regulation of Birth. July 25, 1968.

*Persona Humana:* Declaration on Certain Questions Concerning Sexual Ethics. December 29, 1975.

*Donum Vitae.* Instruction on Respect for Human Life in Its Origin and on the Dignity of Procreation. February 22, 1987.

## Church Documents
## From the U.S. Conference of Catholic Bishops

The following are on the bishops' website, usccb.org:

*Always Our Children: A Pastoral Message to Parents of Homosexual Children and Suggestions for Pastoral Ministers.* September 10, 1997.

*Between Man and Woman: Questions and Answers About Marriage and Same-Sex Unions.* November 2003.

*Follow the Way of Love: A Pastoral Message of U.S. Bishops to Families.* November 17, 1993. Presents the outline of a "spirituality of the family" and includes discussion questions.

*Married Love and the Gift of Life.* November 14, 2006. Provides a brief outline of the Church's teaching on sexual love within marriage and a discussion of contraception and natural family planning.

*Ministry to Persons With a Homosexual Inclination: Guidelines for Pastoral Care.* November 14, 2006. Directives for pastors dealing with homosexual persons.

*Marriage and the Family in the United States: Resources for Society. A Review of Research on the Benefits Generated From Families Rooted in Marriage.* Washington Secretariat of Laity, Marriage, Family Life and Youth. 2012.

## Books

Vincent Genovesi. *In Pursuit of Love: Catholic Morality and Human Sexuality.* Second Edition. Collegeville, MN: Liturgical Press. 1996. This is often used as a seminary textbook and provides a thorough explanation of the Church's teaching with critical analysis.

John S. Grabowski. *Sex and Virtue: An Introduction to Sexual Ethics.* Washington, D.C.: Catholic University of America Press. 2003. Excellent blend of theological, ethical, and scriptural perspectives on human sexuality.

William E. May, Rev. Ronald Lawler, and Joseph Boyle Jr. *Catholic Sexual Ethics: A Summary, Explanation, and Defense.* Second Edition. Huntington, IN: Our Sunday Visitor. 1998. A detailed and rather scholarly summary and defense, providing a solid explanation of the origins and reasoning of Church teaching on sexual ethics.

Kevin O'Neill, CSsR, and Peter Black, CSsR. *The Essential Catholic Handbook: A Guide to Catholic Living.* Liguori. 2003. Intended for average Catholics, this book includes an introduction to basic moral principles and chapters devoted to sexual, medical, and social ethics.

Todd A. Salzman, Michael G. Lawler, and Charles E. Curran. *The Sexual Person: Toward a Renewed Catholic Anthropology.* Washington, D.C.: Georgetown University Press. 2008. A comprehensive treatment from a more philosophical perspective.

Todd A. Salzman and William Lawler. *Sexual Ethics: A Theological Introduction.* Washington, D.C.: Georgetown University Press. 2012.

# Endnotes

1  Denise Lardner Carmody, "Doing Sexual Ethics in a Post-Permissive Society," *The Way* 28 (July 1988) 244-53. Todd A. Salzman and Michael G. Lawler make a similar point when they talk about sex as spiritual: "The love, including the sexual love, shared by a couple in relationship draws them together into communion and this…reflects the communion of the Trinity, draws them closer to God, strengthens their relationship and overflows into all their other relationships." *Sexual Ethics: A Theological Introduction* (Washington, D.C.: Georgetown University Press, 2012) 57-58.

2  Thomas Merton, *Seeds of Contemplation* (Abbey of Gethsemani, Inc., 1961) 25.

3  "A Big Heart Open to God," exclusive interview with Pope Francis by Antonio J. Spadaro, SJ, *America* (September 30, 2013).

4  William E. May, *Sex, Marriage and Chastity: Reflections of a Catholic Layman, Spouse and Parent* (Chicago: Franciscan Herald Press, 1982) 152.

5  A.W. Richard Sipe, *Celibacy: A Way of Loving, Living and Serving* (Liguori, 1996) 25.

6  The Rand Corporation, *Does Watching Sex on TV Influence Teens' Sexual Activity?* (rand.org/pubs/research_briefs)

7  Paul J. Wadell, *Happiness and the Christian Moral Life: An Introduction to Christian Ethics,* revised edition (Lanham, MD: Rowman and Littlefield, 2012) 29-31. See also his earlier book *The Primacy of Love: An Introduction to the Ethics of Thomas*

*Aquinas* (New York, Paulist, 1992), in which he says: "Friendship is a 'certain society,' a miniature community of sorts; in which love and goodness are exchanged...friendships are schools of virtue....Because every friendship is a relationship through which loving and doing good to another makes us better persons. Friendships are schools of virtue because in them we learn well how to practice the good, particularly justice...." Friends practice their love on us and thus bring us into being in a way we could never have accomplished ourselves. Friends see things in us we could never see ourselves, or even if we do see it, they alone know how to draw it out of us. A good friend is someone who draws the best out of us, someone who creates us in the most promising way. That is why a good friend is something like an artist...(69-70)."

8  Charles Blow, "The Demise of Dating," *The New York Times* (December 13, 2008).

9  Laurie Fendrich, "Hooking Up," *The Chronicle of Higher Education* blog (December 13, 2008).

10 "Dorm Brothel: The New Debauchery, and the Colleges That Let It Happen," orthodoxytoday.org/articles6/GuroianCollege.php, accessed April 12, 2013.

11 John Stoltenberg, *Refusing to be a Man: Essays on Sex and Justice* (Portland, OR: Brietenbush Books, Inc., 1989; revised edition, London, UCL Press, 1999) 49.

12 Stoltenberg, 44.

13 "Legislation Creating 'Same-Sex' Marriage: What's at Stake?" (*Catholic New World*, January 6-19, 2013).

14 Philip S. Keane, *Sexual Morality: A Catholic Perspective* (New York: Paulist Press, 1977) 95.

15 John Money, MD, *Gay, Straight and In-Between: The Sexology of Erotic Orientation* (New York: Oxford, 1988).

16 See, for example, Gregory Herek at the University of California-Davis: "For the present discussion, the important point is that many child molesters cannot be meaningfully described as homosexuals, heterosexuals, or bisexuals (in the usual sense of those terms) because they are not really capable of a relationship with an adult man or woman. Instead of gender, their sexual attractions are based primarily on age. These individuals—who are often characterized as fixated—are attracted to children, not to men or women." psychology.ucdavis.edu/rainbow/html/facts_molestation.html, accessed April 12, 2013.

17 A poll by the Pew Research Center in March 2013 notes a significant change in attitudes toward gay marriage, which seems to include a change in attitudes about homosexuality itself. The report notes that in 2003, 58 percent of those polled were opposed to gay marriage and 33 percent were in favor. Ten years later, 49 percent support it and 44 percent were opposed. Among millennials born after 1980, the percentage of those in favor was near 70 percent. Polls do not determine morality, of course, but this research shows that something has caused a significant shift in attitudes.

18 Synopsis from Wikipedia.

19 Naomi Wolf, "Our Bodies, Our Souls: Rethinking Pro-Choice Rhetoric," *The New Republic* (October 16, 1995) 26-35.

20 "Beyond the Stalemate: Forty Years after 'Roe,'" *Commonweal* (June 3, 2013).

21 Francis W. Nichols, "Sexuality Fully Human," *The Furrow* (March 1983).

22 Ronald Rolheiser, *The Holy Longing: The Search for Christian Spirituality* (New York: Doubleday, 1999) 198.

23 William E. May, Rev. Ronald Lawler, Joseph Boyle Jr., *Catholic Sexual Ethics: A Summary, Explanation and Defense,* Second Edition (Huntington, IN: Our Sunday Visitor, 1998) 126.

24 Sipe, *Celibacy,* 133.

CPSIA information can be obtained
at www.ICGtesting.com
Printed in the USA
FFOW05n1533110314